Marxism and history

Two essays

Chris Harman is a leading member of the Socialist Workers Party and the editor of *Socialist Worker*. He is the author of many articles, pamphlets and books including *Class Struggles in Eastern Europe*, *Explaining the Crisis*, *The Fire Last Time: 1968 and After*, *Economics of the Madhouse*, *How Marxism Works* and *The Lost Revolution: Germany 1918 to 1923*.

Marxism and history

Two essays

by

Chris Harman

BOOKMARKS

London, Chicago and Sydney

Marxism and history: two essays – Chris Harman
First published in *International Socialism* 32 and 45
This edition first published 1998
Bookmarks Publications Ltd, c/o 1 Bloomsbury Street , London WC1B 3QE,
England
Bookmarks, PO Box 16085, Chicago, Illinois 60616, USA
Bookmarks, PO Box A338, Sydney South, NSW 2000, Australia
Copyright © Bookmarks Publications Ltd

ISBN 1 898876 31 2

Printed by BPC Wheatons Ltd, Exeter
Cover by Sherbourne Design

**Bookmarks Publications Ltd is linked to an international grouping of
socialist organisations:**
- **Australia:** International Socialist Organisation, PO Box A338, Sydney South
- **Britain:** Socialist Workers Party, PO Box 82, London E3
- **Canada:** International Socialists, PO Box 339, Station E, Toronto, Ontario
  M6H 4E3
- **Cyprus:** Ergatiki Demokratia, PO Box 7280, Nicosia
- **Czech Republic:** Socialisticka Solidarita, PO Box 42, Praha 42, 140 02
- **Denmark:** Internationale Socialister, Postboks 642, 2200 København N
- **Greece:** Socialistiko Ergatiko Komma, c/o Workers Solidarity, PO Box 8161,
  Athens 100 10
- **Holland:** Internationale Socialisten, PO Box 92025, 1090AA, Amsterdam
- **Ireland:** Socialist Workers Party, PO Box 1648, Dublin 8
- **New Zealand:** Socialist Workers Organisation, PO Box 8851, Auckland
- **Norway:** Internasjonale Socialisterr, Postboks 5370, Majorstua, 0304 Oslo 3
- **Poland:** Solidarność Socjalistyczna, PO Box 12, 01-900 Warszawa 118
- **South Africa:** Socialist Workers Organisation, PO Box 18530, Hillbrow
  2038, Johannesburg
- **Spain:** Socialismo Internacional, Apartado 563, 08080, Barcelona
- **United States:** International Socialist Organization, PO Box 16085, Chicago,
  Illinois 60616
- **Zimbabwe:** International Socialist Organisation, PO Box 6758, Harare

Contents

1 Base and superstructure 7

Mechanical materialism and its aftermath 9

The reaction against determinism 11

The revolutionary materialist alternative 14

Production and society 14

Social production 16

Exploitation and the superstructure 19

The key role of changes in production 22

Base, superstructure and social change 25

Base and superstructure under capitalism 30

Superstructure and ideology 32

False consciousness 35

Ideology and class society 37

Ideology and science 38

Ideology and the superstructure 40

Our theory and theirs 41

The central role of class struggle 43

The role of the party in history 47

2 From feudalism to capitalism 55

The scope of the transition 56

Explanations for the transition 58

The arguments of Dobb 62

Brenner's arguments 65

The rival theories: the unity of opposites 73

Expansion rooted in the feudal mode of production ... 75

The growth of the feudal forces of production 79

Trade, the towns and medieval industry 81

Town, country and feudalism 83

Merchants and capitalism 86

The crisis of feudalism 93

The transitional society and the absolutist state 97

The class struggle and the transition 100

The transition and ideology 102

The transition and the first great revolutions 103

Capitalism and colonies 106

Between two revolutions 107

Conclusion 111

1

Base and superstructure

In the social production of their life, men enter into definite relations that are independent of their will, relations of production which correspond to a definite stage of development of their material productive forces.

The sum total of these relations of production constitutes the economic structure of society, the real basis on which rises a legal and political superstructure and to which correspond definite forms of social consciousness.

The mode of production of material life conditions the social, political and intellectual life process in general.

It is not the consciousness of men that determines their being, but, on the contrary, their social being that determines their consciousness.

At a certain stage in their development the material productive forces of society come into conflict with the existing relations of production or—what is but a legal expression for the same thing—the property relations within which they have been at work hitherto.

From forms of development of the productive forces these relations turn into fetters. Then begins an epoch of social revolution.

With the change of the economic foundation the entire immense superstructure is more or less rapidly transformed.

In considering such transformations, a distinction should always be made between the material transformation of the material conditions of production, which can be determined with the precision of natural science, and the legal, political, religious, aesthetic or philosophical—in short ideological—forms in which men become conscious of the conflict and fight it out.

...We do not judge a period of transformation by its consciousness; on the contrary this consciousness must itself be explained from the contradictions of material life, from the existing conflicts between the social productive forces and the relations of production.

In broad outlines Asiatic, ancient, feudal, and modern bourgeois modes of production can be designated as progressive epochs in the economic foundation of society [Karl Marx: from the Preface to *A Contribution to the Critique of Political Economy*].

There is a confusion at the very centre of Marxism. Marx and Engels provided a method of analysing society which has been of enormous fecundity. This has been shown in every generation since the method was first outlined in *The German Ideology* in 1846. Every pronouncement of the 'death of Marxism' by bourgeois ideologues has been proved wrong within a decade or so by a new range of Marxist studies of society, the economy and history. Yet when it has come to spelling out what exactly is the Marxist approach there has been enormous confusion, with 'Marxists' saying apparently contradictory things.

The confusion centres around the couplet 'base' and 'superstructure'. Marx wrote in the Preface to *A Contribution to the Critique of Political Economy* of 1857 that 'the economic structure of society' forms the 'real basis' on which 'rises a legal and political superstructure'.[1]

Ever since then, Marxists have been arguing about the statement. What is the 'base'? The economy? The forces of production? Technology? The relations of production? What is included in the superstructure? Obviously the state. But what about ideology (and revolutionary theory)? The family? The state when it owns industry?

Finally, what is the relation between the 'base' and the 'superstructure'? Does the base determine the superstructure? If so, what exactly is the nature of the determination? And does the superstructure have a degree of 'autonomy'—and if so, how can this be reconciled with talk of 'determination' (even if it is only 'determination in the last resort')?

Mechanical materialism and its aftermath

The answers given to these questions lead to very different views about how society develops.

At the one extreme, there is the view that the base is the forces of production, that they inevitably advance, and that this in turn leads to changes in society.

Political and ideological struggle is then seen as playing no real role. Human beings are products of their circumstances, and history proceeds completely independently of their will. The outcome of wars, revolutions, philosophical arguments or whatnot is always determined in advance. It would have made not one iota of difference to history if Robespierre had walked under a carriage in 1788 or if the sealed train had crashed in April 1917.

This view of Marxism is based upon a certain reading of Marx himself, in particular upon a powerful polemical passage in *The Poverty of Philosophy*:

> In acquiring new productive forces, men change their mode of production; and in changing their mode of production, in changing their way of earning a living, they change all their social relations. The handmill gives you society with a feudal lord; the steam mill society with an industrial capitalist.[2]

It is in the years after Marx's death that such a mechanical, determinist view of history comes to be regarded as 'Marxist' orthodoxy. It was during this period that Marxism came to hegemonise the German workers' movement, and through it the Second International. But it was Marxism as seen through the eyes of Karl Kautsky, the 'Pope of Marxism'.

For Kautsky, historical development had inevitably produced each mode of production in turn—antiquity, feudalism, capitalism—and would eventually lead to socialism. There was an 'inevitable...adaptation of forms of appropriation to forms of production'.[3] Revolutionary movements could not alter this pattern of development. Thus the Hussites of the 15th century and the revolutionary Anabaptists of the 16th century had been able to fight courageously and to present the vision of a new society; but, for Kautsky, they could not alter the inevitable development of history:

> The direction of social development does not depend on the use of peaceful methods or violent struggles. It is determined by the progress and needs of the methods of production. If the outcome of violent revolutionary struggles does not correspond to the intentions of the revolutionary combatants, this only signifies that these intentions stand in opposition to the development of the needs of production.
>
> Violent revolutionary struggles can never determine the direction of social development, they can only in certain circumstances accelerate their pace...[4]

The task of revolutionary socialists under modern capitalism was not to try to cut short the historical process, but simply to reflect its development by carefully building up socialist organisation until capitalism was ready to turn into socialism. But, at the same time, counter-revolutionaries could not stop the onward march of the forces of production and, therefore, of historical evolution. Kautsky insisted that 'regression' from more advanced to more backward forces of production never occurred.[5] 'Economic development', said his most influential work, his introduction to the German Social Democratic Party's *Erfurt Programme*, 'will lead inevitably to the...conquest of the government in the interests of the [working] class'.[6]

Very close to Kautsky's formulations were those of the pioneer Russian Marxist, Plekhanov. He held that the development of production automatically resulted in changes in the superstructure. There is no way human endeavour can block the development of the forces of production. 'Social development' is a 'process expressing laws'.[7] 'The final cause of the social relationships lies in the state of the productive forces.' 'Productive forces...determine...social relations, ie economic relations'.[8]

He provides a 'formula' which sets out a hierarchy of causation in history. The 'state of the productive forces' determines the 'economic relations' of society. A 'socio-political system' then develops on this 'economic basis'. 'The mentality of men living in society [is] determined in part directly by the economic conditions obtaining and in part by the entire socio-political system that has arisen on that foundation.' Finally, the 'various ideologies...reflect the properties of that mentality'.[9]

He would assert that 'history is made by men', but then go on to insist that 'the average axis of mankind's intellectual

development' runs 'parallel to that of its economic development', so that in the end all that really matters is the economic
development.[10]

The outcome of great historical events like the French Revolution did not depend at all on the role played by individuals like
Mirabeau or Robespierre:

> No matter what the qualities of a given individual may be, they
> cannot eliminate the given economic relations if the latter conform
> to the given state of the productive forces.
>
> Talented people can change only individual features of events,
> not their general trend.[11]

Just as Kautsky's interpretation of Marxism dominated in the
parties of the Second International, Plekhanov's was taken up as
the orthodoxy by the Stalinist parties from the late 1920s
onwards.[12] In the hands of Stalin and his 'theoreticians' it
became an unbendable historical law: development of the forces
of production inevitably led to corresponding changes in society, so the growth of industry in Russia would inevitably lead
from a 'workers' state' to 'socialism' and from 'socialism' to
'communism', regardless of the misery and hardship involved;
by contrast, the clearest indication that Western capitalism had
outlived its lifespan was the decline in its forces of production.

The reaction against determinism

Stalinist Marxism did not long outlast Stalin himself. The 'new
left' of the late 1950s and the Maoist left of the mid-1960s both
launched assaults on the crude mechanical determinist account
of history.

They insisted, rightly, that in Marx's own historical writings—
the *Class Struggles in France*, *The 18th Brumaire of Louis
Bonaparte*, *The Civil War in France*—there is not a hint of a passive, fatalistic approach to historical change. They also laid great
emphasis on certain remarks Engels had made in a series of letters he wrote at the very end of his life, in the 1890s, criticising
an overcrude use of historical materialism. Engels had written
to Starkenburg:

> Political, juridical, philosophical, religious, literary, artistic, etc
> development is based on economic development. But these all

11

react on one another and also upon the economic basis. It is not that the economic situation is cause, solely active, while everything else is only passive effect. There is rather interaction on the basis of economic necessity which ultimately always asserts itself.[13]

And to Bloch:

According to the materialist conception of history, the ultimately determining element in history is the production and reproduction of real life. More than that neither Marx nor I have ever asserted. Hence if somebody twists this into saying that the economic element is the only determining one, he transforms that proposition into a meaningless abstract senseless phrase.

The economic situation is the basis, but the various elements of the superstructure—political forms of the class struggle and its results, to wit: constitutions established by victorious classes after a successful battle, etc, juridical forms and even the reflexes of these actual struggles in the brains of the participants, political, juristic, philosophical theories, religious views and their further development into systems of dogmas—also exercise their influence upon the course of the historical struggles and in many cases preponderate in determining their form...

There is an interaction of all these elements in which, amid all the endless host of accidents, the economic element finally asserts itself as necessary.[14]

The post-1956 new left went on to argue that even the terms 'base and superstructure' were simply a metaphor, not to be taken too seriously. The 'reciprocal' influence of the superstructure on the base meant that 'determination' was not to be seen as a strict causal relationship.

The Maoist left did not begin with such an explicit break with the past. The doyen of this school, Louis Althusser, was quite willing in his early 1960s writings to quote Stalin himself favourably.

But the Althusserians created a new theoretical structure which destroyed most of the content of the old notions of 'base', 'superstructure' and 'determination'. Society consisted of a number of different structures—the political, the economic, the ideological, the linguistic—each developing at its own speed, and having an impact on the others. At any particular point in history it could be any one of them that dominated the others. It was only 'in the last instance' that the economic was 'determinant'.

The new left and the Maoist-Althusserian schools were initially very hostile to each other.[15] Yet both of them redefined historical materialism in a way that opened the door to a great dose of voluntarism.

For the 1950s new left, this meant moving away from any tight definition of class or any real concern with how social being might affect social consciousness. In the writings about current events by the most prominent British new left figure, E P Thompson—right through from his 1960 essay 'Revolution'[16] to his anti cruise missile writings of 1980—there is the insistent message that energy and goodwill and a repudiation of tight categories can be enough in themselves to open the road to victory. In his more theoretical writings he rejects the view that 'economic' factors play any sort of determining role in history, or even that they can be separated out from other factors such as the ideological or judicial.[17]

Althusser's tone is different: in his earlier writings the key to change is still a party of an essentially Stalinist sort. But there is the same element of voluntarism as in Thompson: if only the party understands the articulation of the different structures, it can force the pace of history, regardless of 'economic' factors.

Most of his followers have abandoned any notion of 'determination', even in 'the last instance', and have moved to positions that deny any possibility of understanding how societies change. So, for instance, one English post-Althusserian, Gareth Stedman Jones, now tells us that the only way to understand any ideology is in its own terms and that you must not make any attempt to interpret its development in terms of the material circumstances of those who adhere to it.[18] We are right back to the old empiricist adage, 'Everything is what it is and nothing else.' Such is the mouse that the elephantine structures of Althusserianism have given birth to.

The convergence of the old new left and the Althusserians has created a sort of 'common sense' among Marxists which holds that any talk of base and superstructure is really old hat. So widespread has the influence of this 'common sense' been that it has even affected people who reject completely the political conclusions of Thompson or Althusser.[19]

The only concerted resistance to this tendency has come from admirers of the orthodox analytical philosopher G A Cohen.[20] But his defence of Marx involves a complete retreat to the mechanical interpretation of Kautsky and Plekhanov.

13

The revolutionary materialist alternative

Historically, however, there has always been a revolutionary alternative to either mechanical materialism or voluntarism. It existed in part even in the heyday of Kautskyism in some of the writings of Engels and in the work of the Italian Marxist, Labriola.[21]

But the need for a theoretical alternative did not become more widely apparent until the years of the First World War and the Russian Revolution proved the bankruptcy of Kautskyism. It was then that Lenin reread Hegel and concluded, 'Intelligent (dialectical) idealism is closer to intelligent materialism than stupid (metaphysical) materialism'.[22]

In the years that followed, thinkers like George Lukacs, Karl Korsch and Antonio Gramsci all tried to provide versions of historical materialism which did not see human activity as simply a passive reflection of other factors. And in his magnificent *History of the Russian Revolution*, Leon Trotsky provided an account of a world historical event which placed massive emphasis on subjective as well as objective factors—and was criticised from a Plekhanovite point of view for doing so.[23]

A non-mechanical, non-voluntarist version of historical materialism is absolutely vital today. It can easily be found in the works of Marx himself, if you supplement his classic account in the Preface to *A Contribution to the Critique of Political Economy* with what he says at various points in *The German Ideology*, *The Poverty of Philosophy*, *The Communist Manifesto*, and elsewhere.

Production and society

Marx first sets out his account of historical materialism in *The German Ideology* of 1846.

He starts from a materialist recognition that human beings are biologically part of nature:

> The premises from which we start are not dogmas, but real premises from which abstraction can only be made in the imagination. They are real individuals, their activity and the material conditions under which they live, both those which they find existing and those which they produce by their own activity.

> The first fact to be established is the physical organisation of these individuals and their consequent relationship to the rest of nature... The writing of history must always set out from these natural bases and their modification in the course of history through the actions of men.
>
> We must begin by stating the first real premise of human existence, and therefore of all human history, the premise that men must be able to live in order to 'make history'. But life involves before everything else eating and drinking, a habitation, clothing and many other things.
>
> [This is] a fundamental condition of all human history which today as thousands of years ago must be daily and hourly fulfilled merely in order to sustain human life.[24]

So there is a core activity at any point in history which is a precondition for everything else which happens. This is the activity of work on the material world in order to get food, shelter and clothing.

The character of this activity depends upon the concrete material situation in which human beings find themselves.

This determines the content of the most basic forms of human action. And so it also determines what individuals themselves are like.

> The mode of production must not be considered simply as being the reproduction of the physical existence of the individuals. Rather it is a definite form of activity of these individuals, a definite form of expressing their life, a definite mode of life on their part.
>
> As individuals express their life so they are. What they are therefore coincides with their production, both of what they produce and how they produce.
>
> The nature of individuals thus depends on the material circumstances determining their production...[25]

These passages cannot be properly understood unless Marx's central point about human activity—best expressed in the *Theses on Feuerbach* (written at the same time as *The German Ideology*) —is understood. For Marx humanity is part of nature. It arises as a product of biological evolution, and one must never forget its physical dependence on the material world around it. All of its institutions, ideas, dreams and ideals can only be understood as

15

arising from this material reality—even if the route through which they so arise is often long and circuitous. As Labriola put it, 'Ideas do not fall from heaven and nothing comes to us in a dream'.[26]

But that does not mean humans are not qualitatively distinct from the rest of nature. Like any other species, humanity has its own defining features. For Marx the key such defining features are that human beings have to react back upon the material circumstances in which they find themselves in order to survive:

> Men can be distinguished from animals by consciousness, by religion or anything else you like. They distinguish themselves from animals as soon as they begin to produce their means of subsistence, a step which is conditioned by their physical organisation. By producing their means of subsistence men are indirectly producing their actual material life.[27]

Humans cannot act independently of their circumstances. But this does not mean they can be reduced to them. They are continually involved in 'negating' the material objective world around them, in reacting upon it in such a way as to transform both it and themselves.

At each point in history, human beings have to find some way to cope with the needs of material survival. How they cope is not something independent from the objective physical world; rather it is a product of that world. Yet it can never be grasped simply as a mechanical consequence of the physical constitution of nature. It is not mechanical causality, but human action which mediates between the world in which human beings find themselves and the lives they lead.

Social production

Production is never individual production. It is only the collective effort of human beings that enables them to get a livelihood from the world around them.

So the central core activity—work—has to be organised socially. Every particular stage in the development of human labour demands certain sorts of social relationships to sustain it.

In *The German Ideology* Marx refers to the social relations between people at any particular point in history as the 'form of intercourse'. And he insists that, 'The form of intercourse is again determined by production'.[28]

The various institutions that embody human relationships can only be understood as developing out of this core productive interaction:

> The fact is that definite individuals who are productively active in a definite way enter into these definite social and political relations… The social structure and the state are continually evolving out of the life processes of definite individuals, but of individuals, not as they appear in their own or other people's imaginations, but as they really are; ie as they operate, produce materially and hence as they work under definite material limits, presuppositions and conditions independent of their will.[29]

In order to maintain their material lives, human beings are forced to act on the world in certain ways—to engage in material production. But that requires certain forms of cooperation between them.

These core relationships provide a framework which everything else humans do has to fit on to. Everything else is, in this sense, based on them. They provide the limits to what is possible in any society.

So, for instance, a hunter-gatherer society does not have the means to store food for more than a few days, and can only survive if its members are continually on the move looking for more foodstuffs. It is therefore restricted in a number of ways: it cannot be made up of bands of more than 20 or so people; the women in it cannot bear more than one child every four or five years, since the children have to be carried when the band looks for food; there is no means by which one section of society could be freed from labour in order to engage in writing, reading, higher arithmetic, etc.

This is the narrowest way in which you can grasp Marx's argument. But he sees it as having even wider implications than this. The relations of material production not only limit the rest of relations in society, they are also the source of the content of these wider relations as well.

The history of society is the history of changes in the ways in which production takes place, each associated with changes in the relations between human beings immediately around the productive process. And these changes in turn then exert a pressure on all the other social relations.

If, for instance, a band of hunter-gatherers adopts a means of radically increasing the food available to them (by, say, planting root vegetables for themselves instead of having to search for them) and of storing food for long periods of time (for instance, in earthenware pots), this necessarily changes their social relations with each other. Instead of continually moving, they have to stay in one spot until the crop can be harvested; if they are staying in one spot, there is no longer any necessity for restriction on the number of children per woman; the crop becomes something which other bands of people can seize, so providing, for the first time, an incentive for warfare between rival bands.

Changes in the way material production takes place lead to changes in the relations of society in general.

And even relations between people which do not arise out of production—the games people play with each other, the forms sex takes, the relations of adults and young babies—will be affected.

Marx does not at all deny the reality of relations other than directly productive ones. Nor does he deny that they can influence the way production itself takes place. As he puts it in *Theories of Surplus Value*:

> All circumstances which…affect man, the subject of production, have greater or lesser effect upon his functions and activities, including his functions and activities as creator of material wealth, of commodities. In this sense it can be truly asserted that all human relations and functions, however and wherever they manifest themselves, influence material production and have a more or less determining effect upon it.[30]

This is even true in pre-class societies. There is a tendency for old patterns of working and living to crystallise into relatively inflexible structures. They become 'sanctified' with the development of systems of religion, magic, taboos, rituals and so on. At first these systems are carried on even in 'bad times', when the short term needs or desires of the individual might lead to actions which ruin the long term interests of the social collectivity. But, by this very fact, they discourage innovation and moves to new forms of production which would be of long term as well as short term benefit.

18

Exploitation and the superstructure

Something more is needed than simple cooperation between people for the forces of production to develop beyond a certain point. Exploitation is also needed.

While the surplus left after the satisfaction of everyone's minimal needs is small, resources can only be gathered together for further development of the forces of production if the surplus is controlled by a small, privileged minority of society. Hence it is that wherever there is the development of agriculture proper out of horticulture, the growth of trade, the use of dams and canals for flood prevention and irrigation, the building of towns, there are also the beginnings of a polarisation within society between those who exploit and those who are exploited.

The new exploiting group has its origins in its role in production: it is constituted out of those who were most efficient in introducing new methods of agricultural production, or those who pioneered new sorts of trade between one society and its neighbours, or those who could justify themselves not engaging in backbreaking manual labour because of their ability to foresee flood patterns or design waterworks. But from the beginning the new exploiting group secures its control by means other than its role in production. It uses its new wealth to wage war, so further enhancing its wealth through booty and the taking of slaves. It establishes 'special bodies of armed men' to safeguard its old and its new wealth against internal and external enemies. It gains control of religious rites, ascribing the advance of the social productive force to its own 'supernatural powers'. It rewrites old codes of behaviour into new sets of legal rules that sanctify its position.

The new exploiting group, in short, creates a whole network of non-productive relations to safeguard the privileged position it has gained for itself. It seeks through these political, judicial and religious means to secure its own position. It creates a non-economic 'superstructure' to safeguard the source of its own privileges in the economic 'base' .

The very function of these 'non-economic' institutions means that they have enormous economic impact. They are concerned with controlling the base, with fixing existing relations of exploitation, and therefore in putting a limit on changes in the relations of production, even if this also involves stopping further development of the productive forces.

In ancient China, for example, a ruling class emerged on the basis of certain sorts of material production (agriculture involving the use of hydraulic installations) and exploitation. Its members then sought to preserve their position by creating political and ideological institutions. But in doing so they created instruments that could be used to crush any new social force that emerged out of changes in production (eg out of the growth of handicrafts or trade). On occasions that meant physically destroying the new productive means.

So great is the reciprocal impact of the 'superstructure' on the base, that many of the categories we commonly think of as 'economic' are in fact constituted by both. So, for instance, 'property rights' are judicial (part of the superstructure) but regulate the way exploitation takes place (part of the base).

The way the political and judicial feed back into the economic is absolutely central to Marx's whole approach. It is this alone which enables him to talk of successive, distinct 'modes of production'—stages in history in which the organisation of production and exploitation is frozen in certain ways, each with its distinctive ruling class seeking to mould the whole of society to fit in with its requirements.

Far from ignoring the impact of the 'superstructure' on the 'base', as many ignorant critics have claimed for more than a century, Marx builds his whole account of human history around it.

Old relations of production act as fetters, impeding the growth of new productive forces. How? Because of the activity of the 'superstructure' in trying to stop new forms of production and exploitation that challenge the monopoly of wealth and power of the old ruling class. Its laws declare the new ways to be illegal. Its religious institutions denounce them as immoral. Its police use torture against them. Its armies sack towns where they are practised.

The massive political and ideological struggles that arise as a result, decide, for Marx, whether a rising class, based on new forces of production, displaces an old ruling class. And so it is an absolute travesty of his views to claim that he 'neglects' the political or ideological element.

But the growth of superstructural institutions not only freezes existing production relations, it can also have profound effects on the relations between the members of the ruling class themselves, and therefore on the way they react to the other classes in society.

Those who command the armies, the police and the priesthoods live off the surplus obtained by exploitation just as much as do the direct exploiters. But they also develop particular interests of their own: they want their share of the surplus to be as great as possible; they want certain sorts of material production to take place to suit the particular needs of their institutions; they want their sort of lifestyle to be valued more highly than that of those involved in direct production.

Their attempt to gain their own particular aims can lead to the building of ever more complex institutions, to elaborate rules about social behaviour, to endless battles for place and influence. The end result can be labyrinthine structures in which the source of wealth and privilege in material production is completely forgotten.

When this happens, the superstructure can go beyond simply freezing the economic activities on which it is based. It can become a drain on them that prevents their reproduction—and, in doing so, destroys the resources upon which the whole of society, including the superstructure itself, depends. Then material reality catches up with it and the whole social edifice comes tumbling down.

But none of these developments take place without massive political and ideological struggles. It is these which determine whether one set of social activities (those of the superstructure) cramp a different set of social activities (those involved in maintaining and developing the material base). It is these which decide, for Marx, whether the existing ruling class maintains its power until it ruins society, or whether a rising class, based on new forms of production, displaces it.

'The history of all hitherto existing society is the history of class struggle', wrote Marx and Engels at the beginning of *The Communist Manifesto*. But the class struggle is precisely the struggle between those who use the political and ideological institutions of the superstructure to maintain their power over the productive 'base' and exploitation, and those who put up resistance to them.

The superstructure exists to defend exploitation and its fruits. Any real fight against the existing structures of exploitation becomes a fight against the superstructure, a political fight. As Lenin put it, 'Politics is concentrated economics.'

21

Marxism does not see political struggle as simply an automatic, passive reflection of the development of the forces of production. It is economic development that produces the class forces that struggle for control of society. But how that struggle goes depends upon the political mobilisation that takes place within each class.

The key role of changes in production.

We are now in a position to reassess Engels' statement that 'the various elements of the superstructure...also exercise their influence on the course of historical struggles and in many cases preponderate in determining their forms'.[31]

Under any form of class rule a range of structures are built up to reinforce and institutionalise exploitation. Those in control of these institutions have interests of their own, which influence everything else which happens in society—including the nature of material production itself.

However, that cannot be the end of the matter, as the 'voluntarist' rendering of Engels' remarks implies. There is still the question of where the superstructural institutions themselves come from. And there is the all important question of what happens if the superstructure develops in such ways as to impede the reproduction of its own material base.

Marx insists that simply to assert that everything in society influences everything—the superstructure the base as well as vice versa—leads nowhere. He takes the point up in *The Poverty of Philosophy*, his polemic against Proudhon, written soon after *The German Ideology*:

> The production relations of society form a whole. M Proudhon considers economic relations as so many social phases engendering one another, resulting one from the other... The only drawback to this method is that when he comes to examine a single one of these phases, M Proudhon cannot explain it without having recourse to all the other relations of society; which relations he has not yet made his dialectical movement engender.[32]

In his writings Marx points to three different consequences of such a view of society as an undifferentiated whole, with everything influencing everything else.

Firstly, it can lead to a view in which the existing form of society is seen as eternal and unchanging (the view which Marx ascribed to bourgeois economists, seeing social relations as governed by 'eternal laws which must always govern society. Thus there has been history, but there is no longer any'; it is the view that underlies the barrenness of the modern pseudo-science of society, sociology).

Secondly, it can lead to viewing the dynamic of society as lying in some mystical force that lies outside society (Hegel's 'world spirit' or Weber's 'rationalisation').

Thirdly, it can lead to the view that what exists today can only be grasped in its own terms, through its own language and ideas, without any reference to anything else (the position of those idealist philosophers who followed Hegel in 19th century Germany, and of more recent thinkers like Collingwood, Winch and the ex-Althusserians).

Marx's way out of this impasse is to locate the one element in the social whole that has a tendency to cumulative development of its own. This is the action of humans in working on their environment to get a living for themselves. Past labour provides the means for increasing the output of present labour: both material means (tools, machines, access to raw materials) and new knowledge. But in adopting the new ways of working, humans also adopt new ways of relating to each other.

These changes will often be so small as to be barely perceptible (a changed relationship between two people here, an additional person engaged in a particular labour process somewhere else). But if they continue, they will bring about systematic molecular change in the whole social structure. The succession of quantitative changes then has a qualitative impact.

Marx does not deny the possibility of changes in other aspects of social life. A ruler may die and be succeeded by another with a quite different personality. People may tire of one game and start playing another. The accident of birth or upbringing may produce a gifted musician or painter. But all such changes are accidents. There is no reason why they should lead to cumulative social change of any sort. They can produce random change in society, but not a dynamic which moves society in any specific direction.

Material production, on the other hand, does have a tendency to move in one direction rather than another. Its output is wealth, the resources that allow lives to be free from material deprivation.

23

And these resources can be piled up in ever greater quantities.

This does not mean that forces of production always develop as Kautsky, Plekhanov and, more recently, G A Cohen have claimed. As we have seen, the clash between new ways of producing and old social relations is a central feature in history.

Marx noted in *The Communist Manifesto* that 'conservation of the old modes of production in unaltered form was the first condition of existence of all earlier industrial classes'.[33] The outcome of the clash between the new and the old did not have to be the defeat of the old. It could be the stifling of the new. There could be the 'mutual destruction of the contending classes'.[34]

'Regression' (from more advanced forms of production to more backward) is far from being exceptional historically. Civilisation after civilisation has collapsed back into 'barbarism' (ie agricultural production without towns)—witness the dead 'cities in the jungle' to be found in Latin America, south east Asia or central Africa; there are several instances of hunter-gatherer peoples who show signs of once having been horticulturalists (eg some tribes of the Amazon).[35] It depends upon the particular, historically developed features of any society whether the new forces of production can develop and the classes associated with them break through. At one extreme, one can imagine societies which have become so sclerotic that no innovation in production is possible (with, for instance, closely circumscribed religious rites determining how every act of production is performed). At the other extreme, there is modern capitalist society where the be all and end all of life is meant to be increasing the productivity of labour.

In fact, most human societies have been somewhere in between. Because human life is harsh, people have wanted to increase the livelihood they can get for a certain amount of labour, even though certain activities have been sanctified and others tabooed. Generally speaking, there has been a very slow development of the forces of production until the point has been reached where a new class begins to challenge the old. What has happened then has depended on the balance of class forces on the one hand, and the leadership and understanding available to the rival classes on the other.

However, even if the development of the forces of production is the exception, not the norm, it does not invalidate Marx's argument. For those societies where the forces of production break through will thrive and, eventually, reach the point of being able to dominate those societies where the forces of production have been stifled. Very few societies moved on from the stage of barbarism to that of civilisation; but many of those that did not were enslaved by those that did. Again feudal barons and oriental despotic gentry were usually able to beat back the challenge of urban tradesmen and merchants; but this did not stop them all being overwhelmed by the wave of capitalism that spread out from the western fringe of Europe in the 18th and 19th centuries.

It did not matter, at the end of the day, how grandiose or elaborate the superstructure of any society was. It rested on a 'base' in material production. If it prevented this base from developing, then the superstructure itself was eventually doomed. In this sense Engels was right to say that the 'economic element finally asserts itself as dominant'.

As a matter of historical fact, the forces of production did succeed in breaking down and transforming the totality of social relations in which they grew up.

Base, superstructure and social change

Much of the confusion which has arisen among Marxists over the interpretation of Marx's Preface to *A Critique of Political Economy* lies in the definition of the 'base' on which 'the legal and political superstructure' rises.

For some people the 'base' has, in effect, been the material interaction of human beings and nature—the forces of production. For others it has been the social relations within which this interaction occurs, the social relations of production.

You can justify any one of these positions if you take particular quotations from the Preface in isolation from the rest of the passage and from Marx's other writings. For at one point he talks of the 'sum total of these relations of production' as 'the real basis on which arises a political and legal superstructure'. But he says earlier that 'relations of production...correspond to a definite form of development of their material productive forces', and he goes on to contrast 'the material transformation of the material conditions of production, which can be determined with the precision of natural science' and 'legal, political, religious, aesthetic, or

25

philosophical forms'. It is the 'material productive forces' which come into conflict with 'the existing relations of production'.

In fact he is not making a single distinction in the *Critique* between 'base' and 'superstructure'. Two distinctions are involved. There is the distinction between the 'forces of production' and the relations of production. And then there is the distinction between the relations of production and the remaining social relations.

The reason for the confusion is this. The 'base' is the combination of forces and relations of production. But one of the elements in this combination is 'more basic' than the other. It is the 'forces of production' that are dynamic, which go forward until they 'come into conflict' with the static 'relations of production'. Relations of production 'correspond' to forces of production, not the other way round.

Of course, there is a certain sense in which it is impossible to separate material production from the social relations it involves. If new ways of working do involve new social relations, then obviously they cannot come into existence until these new social relations do.

But, as we saw above, there are reasons for assigning priority to the forces of production. Human groups who succeed in changing the ways they work in order to develop the forces of production will be more successful than those that don't. Small, cumulative changes in the forces of production can take place, encouraging changes in the relation between people which are just as small but also just as cumulative. People change their relations with each other because they want to produce the means of livelihood more easily: increasing the means of livelihood is the aim, changes in the social relations of production the unintended consequence. The forces of production rebel against the existing relations of production, not the other way round.

So, for instance, if hunter-gatherers decide to change their social relations with each other so as to engage in horticulture, this is not primarily a result of any belief that horticultural social relations are superior to hunter-gatherer social relations; it is rather that they want access to the increased material productivity of horticulture over hunting and gathering.

In the same way, it is not preference for one set of relations around the production process rather than another that leads the burghers to begin to challenge feudal society. It is rather that for this particular grouping of people within feudalism, the only way to increase their own control over the means of livelihood (to develop the forces of production under their control) is to establish new production relations.

Even when the way one society is organised changes, because of the pressure of another society on it (as when India was compelled to adopt a European style land tenure system in the 19th century, or when hunter-gatherers have been persuaded by colonial administrators and missionaries to accept a settled agricultural life), the reason the pressure exists is that the other society disposes of more advanced forces of production (which translate into more effective means of waging war). And the 'social relations of production' will not endure unless they are successful in organising material production—in finding a 'base' in material production—in the society that is pressurised into adopting them. Where they do not find such a 'base' (as with the Ik in Northern Uganda) the result can even be the destruction of society.[36]

Expansion of material production is the cause, the social organisation of production the effect. The cause itself can be blocked by the old form of organisation of society. There is no mechanical principle which means that the expansion of material production—and with it the changes in social relations—will automatically occur. But in any society there will be pressures in this direction at some point or other. And these pressures will have social consequences, even if they are successfully resisted by those committed to the old social relations.

The distinction between forces and relations of production is prior to the second distinction, between 'economic base' and the superstructure. The development of the forces of production leads to certain changes in the relations of production. These in turn result in changes in the other relations of society being made, until a whole range of institutions of a non-economic sort help reproduce existing economic relations (and so resist further economic change).

The point of these distinctions is to provide an understanding of how society changes. If the forces of production are static, then there is no reason why any society should undergo systematic change at all. The existing social relations will simply tend to reproduce themselves, so that at most there can be random, accidental changes in the relations of people to each other. Neither the social relations of production nor the wider social relations will provide any impetus to the revolutionary social changes that do occur (eg from societies of small bands to those of settled villages, or from those of medieval feudal manors to those of advanced industrial capitalist cities).

There is a further confusion in some of the discussion on forces and relations of production. This concerns what the 'relations of production' are.

At one point in the Preface Marx equates the social relations of production with property relations. People like Cohen have given this view a central place in their own accounts of historical materialism.

It seems to me to limit the notion of the 'social relations of production' far too much. Much of the power of Marx's account of history lies in the way in which it shows how small changes in the forces of production lead to small, cumulative changes in the social relations arising directly at the point of production, until these challenge the wider relations of society. These small changes might involve new property relations, but in many, many important cases do not.

For instance, an increase in the number of journeymen working for the average master craftsman in a medieval city is not a change in property relations. But it does change the social relations in the town in a way which may have very important implications. Similar considerations apply with many other significant historical developments, from the first planting of seeds by hunter-gatherers to changes in production methods in capitalist countries today.

To sum up the argument so far. There is not one distinction in Marx, but two. The forces of production exert pressure on the existing relations of production. And those in turn come into conflict with the existing superstructure.

Once this is grasped, it is possible to deal with the questions which are sometimes raised as to whether particular institutions belong to the base or the superstructure.

There is a sense in which the questions themselves are misframed. The distinction between base and superstructure is not a distinction between one set of institutions and another, with economic institutions on one side and political, judicial, ideological etc institutions on the other. It is a distinction between relations that are directly connected with production and those that are not.

Many particular institutions include both.

So, for instance, the medieval church was a superstructural institution, defending ideologically existing forms of feudal exploitation. But it acquired such large landholdings of its own that no account of the economic structure of medieval society can ignore it. In the same way, modern capitalist states arose out of the need for 'bodies of armed men' to protect particular capitalist ruling classes. But such protection has rarely been possible without the state intervening directly in production.

In pre-capitalist societies, even the question of the class people belong to comes to depend upon superstructural factors. The attempt to preserve existing relations of production and exploitation leads to elaborate codes assigning every individual to one or other caste or estate. This, in turn, determines the productive activity (if any at all) open to them. As Marx put it: '...when a certain degree of development is reached the hereditary nature of castes is decreed as a social law'.[37] And 'in the estate...a nobleman always remains a nobleman, a commoner a commoner, apart from his other relations, a quality inseparable from his individuality'.[38]

There is a sense in which it is true to say that only in bourgeois society do there exist 'pure' classes—social groupings whose membership depends entirely upon relations to exploitation in the productive process, as opposed to privileges embodied in judicial or religious codes.[39] Of course, these codes had their origin in material exploitation, but centuries of frozen social development have obscured that fact.

The situation with the capitalist family is somewhat similar to that of the medieval church or the modern state. It grew up to preserve and reproduce already existing relations of production. But it cannot do this without playing a very important economic role (in the case of the working class family, organising the vast amount of domestic labour that goes into the physical reproduction of labour power, in the case of the capitalist family defining the way in which property is passed from one generation to the next).[40]

This has led to attempts to assign it to the 'base' because of its economic role.[41] But the distinction between base and superstructure is a distinction between social relations which are subject to immediate changes with changes in the productive forces, and those which are relatively static and resistant to change. The capitalist family belongs to the latter rather than the

29

former category, even in its 'economic' function of reproducing the labour force.

Changes in the way reproduction is organised in general follow changes in the way production takes place. The simple fact is that the 'forces of reproduction' do not have the tendency to cumulative change that the forces of production do. The possible ways of restricting the number of births hardly changed from the hunter-gatherer societies of 30,000 years ago until the 20th century—whether these means were used depended not on the sphere of reproduction at all, but on the sphere of production. (For instance, while a hunter-gatherer society is forced to restrict the number of births, many agricultural societies have an interest in as many births as possible.) The material conditions under which children are reared do change—but as a by-product of material changes taking place elsewhere in society.[42]

Finally, these considerations also enable us to dispose of another argument that is sometimes raised—the claim that all social relations are 'relations of production'.[43]

All parts of any social structure owe their ultimate genesis to the realm of production. But what Marx quite rightly emphasised by talk of the 'superstructure' was that, once generated, some parts of the social structure have the effect of constraining the development of others. The old stand in contradiction to the new. The old form of organisation of the state, for instance, rose out of the needs of exploitation at a certain point in history and has continuing effects on production. But it stands in contradiction to the new relationships that are continually being thrown up by further developments of production. To say that all social relations are 'relations of production' is to paint a picture of social development which ignores this important element of contradiction.[44]

Base and superstructure under capitalism

So far this article has been about the relationship of base and superstructure in general. But there are certain peculiarities about their relation under capitalism that deserve a brief mention.

First is the peculiar effect of relations of production on the forces of production. Marx stresses that, for pre-capitalist societies, the established relations of production tend to retard the forces of production. Under capitalism, by contrast, the survival of each individual capital depends upon expanding the forces of production at its disposal more rapidly than its rivals:

> The bourgeoisie cannot exist without constantly revolutionising the instruments of production and thereby the relations of production and with them the whole relations of society… Constant revolutionising of production, uninterrupted disturbance of all social conditions, everlasting uncertainty and agitation distinguish the bourgeois epoch from all earlier ones [45]

Marx holds that the contradiction between the forces of production and the relations of production still comes to the fore eventually, but in a quite specific way.

The growth of the social productive forces of humanity— increased productivity—involves combining ever greater amounts of past labour to each unit of present labour. Under capitalism this takes the form of an increase in the ratio of investment to the workforce. Investment grows more rapidly than the source of all potential profit, living labour. Yet the mainspring of production in this system is the rate of profit, ie the ratio of profit to investment.

The contradiction between the drive to invest and the low level of profit to sustain investment finds expression, for Marx, in a growing tendency to stagnation in the system, ever greater disproportions between the different elements of the economy, and ever deeper economic crises. For those of us who live in the 20th century, it also means an ever present tendency for economic competition to turn into military conflict, with the threat of the forces of production turning into full fledged forces of destruction.[46]

A second difference lies in the way in which under capitalism there is not only a conflict between the development of economic relations and non-economic constraints on them, but also a conflict between different elements of the economy, some of which are seen by Marx as 'more basic' than others. The source of surplus value lies in the realm of production. But growing out of the realm of production are a whole range of activities to do with the distribution of this surplus between different elements of the capitalist class—the buying and selling of commodities, the credit system, the stock market, and so on. These take on a life of their own in a similar way to the different elements in the political and ideological superstructure, and that

31

life affects what happens in the realm of production. Yet, at the end of the day, they cannot escape the fundamental fact that the surplus they dispose of comes from exploitation at the point of production—something which expresses itself in the sudden occurrence of cyclical crises.

None of this means that the distinction between base and super-structure is redundant under capitalism. What it does mean is that there are even more elements of contradiction in this system than previously. Analysing these concretely is a precondition for knowing the way the system is moving and the possibilities of building a determined revolutionary opposition to it.

Superstructure and ideology

What is the relationship of ideas and ideology to the dichotomy of base and superstructure?

Marx is insistent that ideas cannot be divorced from the social context in which they arise. He says: 'Definite forms of social consciousness *correspond* to...the economic structure, the real basis', 'the mode of production of material life *conditions* the social, political and intellectual life process in general', 'social being...*determines*...consciousness' [my emphases].

To understand these strong assertions you have to understand how Marx sees ideas and language as developing.

Ideas arise, for him, out of the material interaction of human beings with the world and each other:

> The production of ideas of conceptions of consciousness is at first directly interwoven with the material activity and the material intercourse of men, the language of real life. Conceiving, think-ing, the material intercourse of men appear at this stage as the direct efflux of their material behaviour. The same applies to mental production as expressed in the language of politics, laws, morality, religions, metaphysics, etc of a people. Men are the pro-ducers of their conceptions, ideas, etc—real active men, as they are conditioned by the development of their productive forces and the forms of intercourse corresponding to these, up to its fur-thest forms. Consciousness can never be anything else than conscious existence, and the existence of men is their actual life process.[47]

Every idea can be shown to have its origin in the material

activity of humans:

> We set out from real active men and on the basis of this we
> demonstrate the development of the ideological reflexes and
> echoes of this life process. The phantoms of the human brain are
> necessarily sublimates of men's material life process, which can
> be empirically established and which is bound to material pre-
> conditions.[48]

He implies there are a number of stages in the development of
consciousness. Animals do not possess consciousness; at most
they are immediately aware of fleeting impressions around them.
Humans begin to move beyond this stage of immediate awareness only as they begin to interact socially with each other on a
regular basis, in acting collectively to control their environment.
So he argues that it is only when humans have developed to the
stage of 'primary historical relations do we find that man also
possesses "consciousness".'[49]

In the process of acting together to get a livelihood, humans
create for the first time a material medium that enables them to
fix fleeting impressions as permanent concepts:

> From the start the 'spirit' is afflicted with the curse of being 'bur-
> dened' with matter, which here makes its appearance in the form
> of agitated layers of air, sounds, in short in language. Language is
> as old as consciousness, language is practical consciousness that
> exits for other men and for that reason alone it really exists for me
> personally as well; language like consciousness only arises from
> the need, the necessity of intercourse with other men.[50]

Or, as he puts it elsewhere, 'language is the immediate actuality
of thought'.[51]

Knowledge, then, is a social product. It arises out of the need
for communication, which in turn is a product of the need to carry
out social production. Consciousness is the subjective expression
of objectively existing relations. It originates as consciousness of
participation in those relationships. Its embodiment, language, is
a material process which is one of the constituents of these relationships. 'Ideas and thoughts of people, then, are ideas and
thoughts about themselves and of people in general...for it [is]
the consciousness not merely of a single individual but of the
individual in his interconnection with the whole of society'.[52]

Marx's materialism amounts to this. Mind is developed upon

the basis of matter. It depends for its functioning upon the satisfaction of the needs of the human body. It depends for the form of its consciousness upon the real relationships between individuals. The content of the individual mind depends upon the individual's material interaction with the world and other people.

But the human mind cannot simply be reduced to matter. The individual human being who thinks has the ability to act. The subjective develops out of the objective, but is still real.

As Marx put it in the first of the *Theses on Feuerbach*: 'The chief defect of all hitherto existing materialism is that the thing, reality, sensuousness, is conceived only in the form of an object of contemplation, but not as human sensuous activity, not subjectively... Feuerbach does not conceive human activity itself as objective activity.'

However, if Marx asserts the reality of individual thought and activity, he also emphasises their limits. Thought arises from activity. And as soon as the link with activity is broken, thought is seen to lose some of its content: 'Man must prove the truth, ie the reality and power, the this-sidedness of his thinking, in practice.'

So thinking is only 'real' in so far as it has practical application, insofar as it alters the world. There is an objective reality apart from human awareness. But it is only through their activity that humans can make contact with this reality, link their consciousness to it 'The question of whether objective truth can be attributed to human thinking is not a question of theory but is a practical question...the dispute over the reality or non-reality of thinking that is isolated from practice is a purely scholastic question'.[53]

It is in the coming together of humanity and the world in activity that both the reality of the world and the truth of thought are determined.

Marx's historical materialism does not hold that will, consciousness and intention play no part in history. Human action is continually changing the world in which human beings find themselves, and their relationships with each other.

The mechanical materialist Kautskyite interpretation of Marxism makes the very mistake Marx himself ascribes to Feuerbach. It fails to see that history is the history of human activity. But social activity involves consciousness.

It is human beings with particular ideas who invent new
34   tools, challenge existing ways of living, organise revolutionary

movements or fight to defend the status quo. The contradictions between the forces of production and the relations of production, between the base and the superstructure, find expression in arguments, organised disagreements and bitter struggles between people. These are part of the real development of society. To deny that is to present a picture of society in which explosive antagonisms no longer exist.

But consciousness never arises in a void. It is a subjective link between objective processes. The ideas of any individual or group develop on the basis of material reality and feed back into that reality. They cannot be reduced to that reality, but neither can they be divorced from it.

It is this link which enables us to make sense of Marx's notions of 'false consciousness' and 'ideology'.

False consciousness

When people are engaged in material practice they have an immediate awareness of their action and of the part of the world it impinges on which is unlikely to be false. Unless they are blind or deranged they know they are digging into the ground or aiming rifles at other people, or whatnot. At this level their activity and their consciousness coincide. But the content of this consciousness is minimal. In fact it hardly deserves the name 'consciousness' at all.

But alongside such immediate awareness there is always a more general consciousness. This attempts to go beyond that which people immediately know and to provide some overall conception of the context they find themselves in. It tells them, for instance, that they are not simply digging, but are providing themselves with a future livelihood, or that they are not simply aiming their rifles, but are defending their 'fatherland'.

There is no guarantee of the 'truth' or 'reality' of this general consciousness. An economic crisis can mean that, however hard you dig, you won't be able to sell the crop you grow and gain a livelihood; your rifle may be defending the profits of a multinational, not some alleged 'fatherland'.

Whereas immediate consciousness is part and parcel of your activity and therefore must be 'real' in certain very limited senses, general consciousness can be no more than a blind accompaniment to activity. In this sense it finds no expression in the world. It has, in Marx's words, no 'this-sidedness' and no 'reality'. Or the outcome of the activity it guides is different to what is expected. Its objective content is different to its subjective content. It is at best partially 'real'.[54]

Yet Marx is insistent that even 'false' general consciousness originates in real activity. So in criticising one particular form of 'unreal' consciousness, the 'German' ideology of idealist philosophy, he writes:

> The philosophers would only have to dissolve their language into the ordinary language from which it is abstracted to recognise it as the distorted language of the actual world and to realise that neither thought nor language in themselves form a reality of their own, that they are only manifestations of actual life...
>
> For philosophers one of the most difficult tasks is to descend from the world of thought to the actual world. Language is the immediate actuality of thought. Just as philosophers have given thought an independent existence, so they had to make language into an independent realm. This is the secret of philosophical language in which thoughts in the form of words have their own context. The problem of descending from the world of thoughts to the actual world is turned into the problem of descending from language to life.[55]

> We have seen that the whole problem of the transition from thought to reality, hence from language to life, exists only in philosophical illusion.[56]

Such a view of abstract philosophical thought leads straight to the contempt for it expressed in the *Theses on Feuerbach*: 'Social life is essentially practical. All the mysteries which mislead theory into mysticism find their rational solution in human practice and in the contemplation of this practice.'

On the face of it, the view he puts forward is very close to that of philosophers who have denied any possibility of general philosophical, social or historical notions. Thus the linguistic philosophy of Wittgenstein claims that all the traditional problems of philosophy arise because philosophers have taken the concepts of ordinary life and used them out of context.[57]

In a somewhat similar way 'historicist' thinkers have insisted that no idea or social practice can be understood outside the particular historical and cultural context in which it is found; any attempt at a wider explanation must be false.[58]

But Marx's view is very different to these. They see false notions as arising as a result of the strange desire of philosophers to generalise, of a weird 'mental cramp' which afflicts people. And they conclude that all generalisation is wrong.

Marx, by contrast, sees false generalisation, the result of the divorce of theory from practice, as itself having material roots. Only in a society without classes can the general notions develop straight out of the immediate experiences of people, without distortion. For everyone in society is then involved in a single, shared cooperative activity .

Ideology and class society

Once there is a division between exploiting and exploited classes, and, based on that, a growing division between mental and manual labour, the single practice disintegrates and with it, the possibility of a single view of the world.

In a class society the social whole is continually rent asunder by the clash between the development of the forces of production and the existing relations of production, a clash which finds expression in the struggle between different social groups.

Different groups will have different practical aims, some in the preservation of existing social relations, some in their overthrow so as to allow the development of new social relations based upon new forces of production. The result is that different sections of society have different experiences of social reality. Each will tend to develop its own overall view of society, which will be markedly different to that developed by the others.

Such views are not only accounts of what society is like. They also serve to bind people together for the practical task of preserving or transforming society, for each prioritises some sorts of practical social activity to the detriment of others.

It is only in the minds of certain empiricist philosophers that description and prescription, fact and value are distinct. What is 'good' or 'valuable' from the point of view of one social group and its activity will be 'bad' for another social group. What one section of society sees as essential to the preservation of social life, because it preserves the existing relations of production, will be seen as bad by another because it obstructs the development of new forces of production. Categories which were previously unproblematic, simply descriptions of what was necessary to maintain society and human life, become prescriptions expressing the desires of different, opposed groups.

The struggle for social domination between the different groups is, in part, a struggle by each to impose its view of society, its way of organising social activity, upon the others. It has to assert that its notions are 'true' and the others 'false'; or at least to show that the meaning given by other social groups to their activities can be subordinated to its own overall visions of the world.

The attempt of philosophers to measure rival conceptions of the world against a single loadstone of 'truth' is part of this struggle. They attempt to generalise the experience of a particular class in such a way as to enable it to dominate the thinking of other classes. But because of the real contradictions between the experiences and interests of different classes, this is an endless quest. Any philosophical view can always be countered by another, since each has roots in the contradictory experiences of material life. That is why every great philosophy eventually slides into mysticism.

But this does not mean, for Marx, that different views of the world are equally valid (or equally false). For some provide a more comprehensive view of society and its development than others.

A social group identified with the continuation of the old relations of production and the old institutions of the superstructure necessarily only has a partial view (or a series of partial views) of society as a whole. Its practice is concerned with the perpetuation of what already exists, with 'sanctifying' the accomplished fact. Anything else can only be conceived as a disruption or destruction of a valuable, harmonious arrangement. Therefore, even at times of immense social crisis, its picture of society is one of a natural, eternally recurring harmony somehow under attack from incomprehensible, irrational forces.

Ideology and science

A rising social group, associated with an advance of the productive forces, has a quite different approach. At first, at least, it has no fear of new forms of social activity which disrupt the old relations of production and their superstructure along with it. It identifies with and understands these new forms of activity. Yet, at the same time, because it is also in collision with the old order, it has practical experiences of that as well. It can develop some sort of view of society which sees how all the different elements fit together, the forces of production and the relations of production, the base and the superstructure, the oppressed class and the oppressing class.

Because it has a practical interest in transforming society, its general ideas do not have to be either a blind commentary on events or a mysticism aimed simply at preserving the status quo. They can be a source of real knowledge about society. They can act not just as a banner to rally people behind, but as a guide to effective action. They can be scientific, despite their origin in the practice of one social group.

Marx certainly thought this was the case with classical political economy. Again and again he refers to the 'scientific' merit of the writings of Adam Smith and David Ricardo, and even of some of the mercantilist and physiocratic economists who preceded them.

They were 'scientific' because they tried to cut through the superficial appearances of society to grasp the 'inner connections between the economic categories—or the hidden structure of the bourgeois economic system', 'to attempt to penetrate the inner physiology of bourgeois society...'[59]

This 'esoteric' approach, which looks to the underlying social reality, is in marked contrast with a simply 'exoteric' approach which takes for granted the existing external social forms. The classical political economists never succeed fully in breaking with the 'exoteric' method, but they begin to move in that direction, and in doing so lay the basis for a scientific understanding of the inner structure of capitalism.

Their ability to develop a scientific understanding is related to the class they identify with—the rising industrial capitalists. Marx described Smith, for instance, as 'the interpreter of the frankly bourgeois upstart',[60] writing in 'the language of the still revolutionary bourgeoisie, which ,has not yet subjected to itself the whole of society, the state, etc'.[61]

Because the industrial capitalists do not yet control society, they have to adopt a critical view of its external features, to seek an objective analysis of the extent to which these features fit in with the drive to capital accumulation. This leads to the attempt to locate the production of wealth in the labour process, and to contrast 'productive' labour which creates surplus value with the parasitic functions of the old state, church and so on.

Ideology and the superstructure

The situation changes radically when the rising class has consolidated its hold. Then it no longer has any use for a revolutionary critical attitude towards society as a whole. The only practical activity it is interested in is that which reproduces existing economic and social relations. And so its 'theory' degenerates into attempts to take different superficial aspects of existing society and present them as if they provided general laws about what all societies must be like.

For Marx, 'ideology' is a product of this situation. The dominant social class controls the means by which a distinct layer of people can be freed from physical labour so as to engage in intellectual production. But, dependent upon the ruling class for their sustenance, these 'intellectuals' will tend to identify with it—the ruling class establishes all sorts of mechanisms to ensure that.

Identifying with the ruling class means stopping short of any total critique of existing social relations and taking for granted the form in which they present themselves. The particular aspects of existing society are then seen as self sustaining, as lacking any common root in social production.

So you get a series of separate, self contained disciplines: 'politics', 'neo-classical economics', 'psychology', 'sociology' and so on. Each of these treats aspects of a unitary social development as if they occurred independently of each other. 'History' becomes a more or less arbitrary linking together of events and personages. And philosophy becomes the attempt to overcome the separation of these disciplines through looking at the concepts they use at ever greater degrees of remoteness from the world of material production and intercourse.

Such ways of looking at the world are 'ideological', not because they are necessarily conscious apologetics for the existing ruling class, but because the very way in which they are structured prevents them seeing beyond the activities and ideas which reproduce existing society—and therefore also the ruling class—to the material processes in which these are grounded. They sanctify the status quo because they take the concepts it uses at face value, instead of seeing them as transitory products of social development.

'Ideology' in this sense is linked to the superstructure. It plays about with concepts which arise in the superstructure, seeking to link and derive one from the other, without ever cutting through surface appearances to look at the real process of social production in which the superstructure and its concepts arise.

It is the contradictions of such 'ideological' arguments that can only 'be resolved by the descent from language to life'.

But this descent can only be made by thinkers who identify with a rising class. For they alone are identified with a practice which puts into question all existing social relations, seeking to criticise what happens on the surface of society, linking it to underlying relations of material production and exploitation.

While the thinkers of an established ruling class are confined to continual elaboration in the realm of ideology, the thinkers of a rising class can begin to develop a scientific understanding of social development .

Our theory and theirs

A rising class's thinkers cannot simply proclaim that they have the truth. They have to prove it.

First, they have to show that they can take up and develop the insights which the thinkers of earlier rising classes made. So, for instance, Marx set out in his economic writings not simply to give his explanation of the workings of capitalism, but also to show how he could complete the work of classical political economy by solving problems it had set itself without success.

Second, it has to be able to show how the superficial social features which ideology deals with can be derived from the underlying social processes it describes. As Marx puts it, it has to be able to derive the 'exoteric' from the 'esoteric'. So a scientific Marxist analysis of any society has to be able to provide an understanding of the various ideological currents of that society, showing how they arise out of the real world, expressing certain aspects of it, but in a distorted way.

Finally, at the end of the day, there is only one real test of any science: its ability to guide practice. And so arguments within Marxism itself can only be finally resolved in the course of revolutionary working class struggle.

A very important point underlies all this discussion. Not all ideas about .society are 'ideological'. The scientific understanding

41

which the thinkers of a rising class develop is not. Nor is the immediate awareness which people have of their actions. This only becomes 'ideological' when it is interpreted through a framework of general ideas provided by an established ruling class. By contrast, if it is interpreted through the theory of a rising class, it is on its way to becoming the true self consciousness of a society.

'Ideology' is part of the superstructure in the sense that it is a passive element in the social process, helping to reproduce old relations of production. But revolutionary self consciousness is not. It is an active element, arising out of people's material circumstances, but feeding back into them to change them.

In the real world there are all sorts of hybrid sets of ideas which lie somewhere in between science and ideology, between true and false consciousness. People's experience can be of partial challenges to the existing society. They gain partial insights into the real structure of society, but seek to interpret them through piecemeal adjustments to old ideological frameworks.

Even the output of the ideologies of the existing order cannot be dismissed out of hand. The worst of them cannot completely ignore those experiences of the mass of people which challenge the ruling class's view of the world: their ideological function means they have, somehow, to try to prove that those experiences are compatible with the ruling class's view. So the worst hack journalists or TV commentators have to recognise that there is opposition to the ruling class, reporting on strikes, demonstrations and so on, if only to condemn such struggles and to isolate those involved in them. The worst pulp novelists have to start from some image of ordinary people's lives, however distorted, if they are to find a mass audience. The most reactionary priests are only effective insofar as they can provide illusory relief to the real problems of their parishioners.

This leads to all sorts of contradictions within the ruling ideology. Some of its most prominent proponents can be those who make most efforts to relate to people's lived experiences. The ideology itself encourages 'social scientists', historians, writers, artists and even theologians to make enormous efforts to fit empirical observation and experience into their accounts of reality. But this inevitably leads to contradictory accounts, with some of the ideologues beginning to question some of the tenets of the established ideology. Marx recognised that a great writer or artist is able to reflect all the contradictory experiences that beset people who live in his or her society, and, in the process to begin to go beyond the limits set by his or her class position. In a few cases this even leads them to a break with their own class and to identify with the revolutionary opposition to it.

A scientific understanding of social development demands a complete break with the whole method of the pseudo-social sciences of those who defend the existing social order. But that does not mean that we can neglect the elements of truth that those who practise these disciplines stumble across. Still less can we ignore the often quite profound grasp of the social process to be found in certain non-Marxist historians or in great novelists like Balzac or Walter Scott.

Marxism shows its superiority over bourgeois thought not by simply treating all bourgeois thinkers with contempt, but rather by showing that it can encapsulate the advances made by bourgeois thinkers into its own total view of reality—something which no bourgeois 'social scientist' can do and which no bourgeois thinker has attempted since Hegel.

The central role of class struggle

The Marxist approach begins, then, by pointing to the contradictory ways in which the forces of production and the relations of production, the base and the superstructure, material reality and people's ideas, develop. But none of these contradictions simply resolve themselves, as the mechanical materialists assert. Their resolution only takes place on the basis of the struggles of human beings, of class struggles.

Once you have societies divided between those who produce directly and those who live off a surplus product, any growth of the productive forces, however slow and piecemeal, leads to a corresponding change in the objective weight of the different classes in society. And some ways of developing the productive forces lead to qualitative changes, to new ways of extracting a surplus, to the embryos of new exploiting and exploited classes (and, eventually, to the formation of a class that can run society without exploiting anyone).

But the new ways of producing always face resistance from at least some of those whose interests lie in preservation of the old ways. The advance of every new mode of production is always marked by bitter class wars (even if, as with the religious wars of

43

the 16th and 17th centuries, these ways do not always involve clean breaks between classes, but often complicated, cross-cutting alliances between the most dynamic section of the rising class and certain interest groups within the old order). Whether the new ways of producing break through depends on who wins these struggles. Economic developments are very important in this. They determine the size of the different classes, their geographical concentration (and therefore the ease with which they can be organised), their degree of homogeneity, the physical resources at their disposal.

Such direct economic factors can certainly create a situation in which the rising class cannot gain a victory, whatever it does. The objective balance of forces is too powerfully weighted the other way. But when the objective factors create a situation of near equality of forces for the rival classes, what come to matter are other factors—the ideological homogeneity, the organisation and the leadership of the rival classes.

For the mechanical materialist, ideas are simply an automatic reflection of material being. But in real historical processes of social transformation it is never that simple.

The institutions of the old ruling class are continually trying to define the ways in which people throughout society see themselves and their relations with others. The members of the rising class at first accept these definitions as the only ones available to them: so for instance, the early medieval burghers accepted the precepts of medieval Catholicism in their totality.

But the members of a rising class get involved in practical activity which cannot easily be encompassed by the old definitions. People begin to do things which the old world view says they should not. The institutions that enforce the old world view then threaten punitive action against them.

At this point two options are open. Those involved in the new forms of activity concede to the pressures on them from the old order, and the new forms of activity cease. Or they generalise their clash with the old ideology, developing out of elements of it a new total world view, behind which they attempt to rally all those in a similar objective situation to themselves.

A new system of ideas is not just a passive reflection of economic changes. It is rather a key link in the process of social transformation, mobilising those affected by cumulative small scale changes in production into a force whose aim is to change social relations in their entirety.

Take, for instance, the classic debate on Protestantism and the rise of capitalism. According to opponents of Marxism, like Max Weber, it was the autonomous 'non-economic' development of a new religious ideology which alone provided the ground in which new capitalist ways of producing could take root. Puritanism caused capitalism.

According to the mechanical materialists, it was the other way round. Protestantism was simply a mechanical reflection of the development of capitalist relations. Capitalism was the cause, Protestantism was the effect.

Each missed out a vital link in the chain of historical development. Protestantism developed because some people in a feudal society began to work and live in ways that are not easily reconcilable with the dominant ideology of medieval Catholicism. They began to reinterpret some of its tenets so as to make sense of their new forms of behaviour. But this led to clashes with the ideological guardians of the old order (the church hierarchy). At this point a series of figures emerged who tried to generalise the challenge to the old ideology—Luther, Calvin, etc. Where the challenge was unsuccessful or where those who made it were forced to compromise (as in Germany, France and Italy), the new ways of working and living became no more than marginal elements in a continuing feudal society. But where the challenge was successful (in Britain and the Netherlands) it liberated the new ways of working and living from the old constraints—it generalised bourgeois forms of production.

The same relationship holds between the workers' struggle under capitalism and the ideas of revolutionary socialism.

Initially, workers try to fit their experience of fighting back against aspects of capitalism into ideological frameworks that are bequeathed to them from the past. These frameworks shape the form their struggles take, so that the struggles are never a simple reflection of material interests. 'The deadweight of the past hangs like a nightmare on the brain of the living', as Marx put it.[62] But the process of trying to interpret their new experiences through old frameworks creates a tension within the old frameworks, which is only resolved as people try to change the frameworks.

As Antonio Gramsci put it, 'The active man of the masses works practically, but he does not have a clear, theoretical consciousness of his actions, which is also a knowledge of the world

45

insofar as he changes it.' So there are 'two sorts of consciousness', that 'implicit in his actions', and that 'superficially explicit,
which he has inherited from the past and which he accepts without criticism':

> This 'verbal' conception is not without consequences; it binds him
> to a certain social group, influences his moral behaviour and the
> direction of his will in a more or less powerful way, and it can reach
> the point where the contradiction of consciousness will not permit
> any action... [Therefore] the unity of theory and practice is not a
> given mechanical fact, but a historical process of becoming.[63]

Thus the Chartists of the 1830s and 1840s attempted to come
to terms with new experiences through older, radical democratic
notions. But this created all sorts of contradictory ideological formulations. That was why some of the most popular orators and
writers were people like Bronterre O'Brien, Julian Harvey and
Ernest Jones who began to articulate people's experience in
newer, more explicitly socialist ways.

Marxism itself was not a set of ideas that emerged fully
formed out of the heads of Marx and Engels and then magically
took a grip of the working class movement. The birth of the
theory was dependent on a distillation by Marx and Engels of the
experiences of the young workers' movement in the years prior
to 1848. It has been accepted by workers since then, insofar as it
has fitted in with what struggles were already beginning to teach
them. But its acceptance has then fed back into the struggles to
influence their outcome.

The theory does not simply reflect workers' experience under
capitalism; it generalises some elements of that experience (those
of struggling against capitalism) into a consciousness of the
system as a whole. In doing so, it gives new insights into how to
wage the struggle and a new determination to fight.

Theory develops on the basis of practice, but feeds back into
practice to influence its effectiveness.

The point is important because theory is not always correct
theory. There have historically been very important workers'
struggles waged under the influence of incorrect theories:
Proudhonism and Blanquism in France in the second half of the
19th century; Lassallianism in Germany; Narodnism and even
Russian Orthodoxism in Russia in the years before 1905;
Peronism in Argentina; Catholicism and nationalism in Poland;

and, of course, the terrible twins, social democracy and Stalinism.

In all of these cases workers have gone into struggle influenced by 'hybrid' views of the world—views which combine a certain immediate understanding of the needs of class struggle with a more general set of ideas accepting key elements of existing society. Such a false understanding of society in its totality leads to enormous blunders—blunders which again and again have led to massive defeats.

In the face of such confusion and such defeats, nothing is more dangerous than to say that ideas inevitably catch up with reality, that victory is certain. For this invariably leads to a downplaying of the importance of combining the practical and the ideological struggle.

The role of the party in history

The other side of the coin to the mechanical materialists' downgrading of the ideological struggle has been a tendency for certain socialist academics to treat the ideological struggle as something quite separate from practical conflicts. This is especially true of the reformists of the now defunct *Marxism Today* and of the Labour left.

But the struggle of ideas always grows out of struggle in the world of material practice, where ideas have their root, and always culminates in further such material struggles. It was the everyday activity of craftsmen and merchants under feudalism which gave rise to heretical, Protestant, religious formulations. And it was the all too real activity of armies which fought across the length and breadth of Europe which, at the end of the day, determined the success or failure of the new ideology.

The new idealists often claim their theoretical inspiration from Antonio Gramsci, but he was insistent on the connection between theoretical and practical struggle:

> When the problem of the relation of theory and practice arises, it does so in this sense: to construct on a determined practice a theory that, coinciding and being identified with the decisive elements of the same practice, accelerates the historical process in act, makes the practice more homogeneous, coherent and efficacious in all its elements, that is, giving it the maximum force; or else, given a certain theoretical problem, to organise the essential practical elements to put it into operation.[64]

47

If you want to challenge capitalism's ideological hold today, you cannot do so unless you relate to people whose everyday struggles lead them to begin to challenge certain of its tenets. And if you want to carry the challenge through to the end, you have to understand that the ideological struggle transforms itself into practical struggle.

The transformation of practice into theory and theory into practice does not take place of its own accord. 'A human mass does not "distinguish" itself and does not become independent "by itself" without organising itself, and there is no organisation without intellectuals, that is, without organisers and leaders...'[65]

A rising class develops a clear set of ideas insofar as a polarisation takes place within it, and what is, at first, a minority of the class carrying the challenge to the old ideology through to its logical conclusion.

At a certain stage in the ideological and practical struggle that minority crystallises out as a separate 'party' (whether it calls itself that or not). It is through the struggle of such parties that the development of the forces and relations of production find expression in new ideas, and that the new ideas are used to mobilise people to tear the old superstructure apart. In a famous passage in *What is to be Done?*, Lenin said that 'political ideas' are brought to the working class from outside. If he meant that workers played no part in the elaboration of the revolutionary socialist world view he was wrong.[66] If he meant that practical experience did not open workers up to socialist ideas he was wrong.[67] But if he meant to stress that socialist ideas do not conquer the class without the separation off of a distinct socialist organisation, which is built through a long process of ideological and practical struggle, he was absolutely right.

The famous discussions of the mechanical materialists were about the 'role of the individual in history'.[68] But it was not the individual, but the party, which became central for the non-mechanical, non-voluntaristic materialism of the revolutionary years after 1917.

Trotsky explains in his masterpiece, the *History of the Russian Revolution*, that revolutions occur precisely because the superstructure does not change mechanically with every change in the economic base:

Society does not change its institutions as the need arises the way a mechanic changes his instruments. On the contrary, society

actually takes the institutions which hang upon it as given once
and for all. For decades the oppositional criticism is nothing more
than a safety valve for mass dissatisfaction, a condition of the sta-
bility of the social structure.[69]

The 'radical turns which take place in the course of a revolution' are not simply the result of 'episodic economic disturbances'.
'It would be the crudest mistake to assume that the second revolution [of 1917] was accomplished eight months after the first
owing to the fact that the bread ration was lowered from one and
a half pounds to three quarters of a pound.' An attempt to explain
things in these terms 'exposes to perfection the worthlessness of
that vulgarly economic interpretation of history which is frequently
given out as Marxism'.[70]

What become decisive are 'swift, intense and passionate
changes in the psychology of classes which have already been
formed before the revolution'.[71] 'Revolutions are accomplished
through people, although they be nameless. Materialism does not
ignore the feeling, thinking, acting man, but explains him'.[72]

Parties are an integral part of the revolutionary process:

> They constitute not an independent, but nevertheless a very impor-
> tant element in the process.
>
> Without the guiding organisation, the energy of the masses
> would dissipate like steam not enclosed in a piston box. But nev-
> ertheless, what moves things is not the piston or the box, but the
> steam.[73]

But parties always involve a subjective element in the way that
economic forces and the formation of classes do not. Parties have
to be organised around certain ideological postulates, and that
requires the effort, activity and argument of individuals.

In Russia in 1917 the contradictions in material reality could
not be resolved without the working class seizing power. But
the working class could not become conscious of that need without a minority in the class separating itself off from the ideas of
the majority. There needed to be 'the break of the proletarian van-
guard with the petty bourgeois bloc'.[74] Many workers began to
move, under the pressure of events, to make this break. But they
were held back at first from consummating the break because of
their own confused ideas: 'They did not know how to refuse the
premise about the bourgeois character of the revolution and the

49

danger of the isolation of the proletariat'.[75] 'The dictatorship of the proletariat was to be inferred from the whole situation, but it had still to be established. It could not be established without a party'.[76]

The fact that the human material existed to build a party before 1917 was a result of objective historical developments. But these developments had to find expression in the activity and ideas of individuals. And once the revolution started, the activity of the party was not a blind reflection of reality. True, 'The party could fulfil its mission only by understanding it',[77] but that depended on the ability of different individuals to articulate ideas about the objective situation and to win party members to them.

This was where, for Trotsky, one individual, Lenin, did play an unparalleled role. He was 'needed' for the party to understand events and act effectively. 'Until his arrival, not one of the Bolshevik leaders dared to make a diagnosis of the revolution.'

He was not a 'demiurge of the revolutionary process', acting on it as an arbitrary element from outside. 'He merely entered into the chain of objective historical forces. But he was a great link in that chain.' Without Lenin many workers were beginning to grope towards a knowledge of what needed to be done. But their groping needed to be generalised, to become part of a new total view of the revolution. 'Lenin did not impose a plan on the masses: he helped the masses to recognise and realise their own plan'.[78]

The arguments would have taken place without him. But there is no guarantee they would have been resolved in a way which would have enabled the party to act decisively:

Inner struggle in the Bolshevik Party was absolutely unavoidable. Lenin's arrival merely hastened the process. His personal influence shortened the crisis.

Is it possible, however, to say confidently that the party without him would have found its road? We would by no means make bold to say that. The factor of time is decisive here, and it is difficult in retrospect to tell time historically.

Dialectical materialism at any rate has nothing in common with fatalism. Without Lenin the crisis, which the opportunist leadership was inevitably bound to produce, would have assumed an extraordinarily sharp and protracted character. The conditions of war and revolution, however, would not allow the party a long period for fulfilling its mission. Thus it is by no means excluded that a disoriented and split party may have let slip the revolutionary opportunity for many years.[79]

The individual plays a role in history, but only insofar as the individual is part of the process by which a party enables the class to become conscious of itself.

An individual personality is a product of objective history (experience of the class relations of the society in which he or she grows up, previous attempts at rebellion, the prevailing culture, and so on). But if he or she plays a role in the way a section of the class becomes conscious of itself and organises itself as a party, he or she feeds back into the historical process, becoming 'a link in the historical chain'.

For revolutionaries to deny this is to fall into a fatalism which tries to shrug off all responsibility for the outcome of any struggle. It can be just as dangerous as the opposed error of believing that the activity of revolutionaries is the only thing that matters.

The point is absolutely relevant today. In modern capitalism there are continual pressures on revolutionary Marxists to succumb to the pressures of mechanical materialism on the one hand and of voluntaristic idealism on the other.

Mechanical materialism fits the life of the bureaucracies of the Labour movement. Their positions rest upon the slow accretion of influence within existing society. They believe the future will always be a result of gradual organic growth out of the present, without the leaps and bounds of qualitative change. That is why a Marxism which is adjusted to their work (like that of the former Militant tendency or the pro-Russian wing of the old Communist Party) tends to be a Kautskyite Marxism.

The voluntarism of the new idealism fits in with the aspirations of the new middle class and of reformist intellectuals. They live lives cut off from the real process of production and exploitation, and easily fall into believing that ideological conviction and commitment alone can remove from the world the spectres of crisis, famine and war.

Revolutionary Marxism can only survive these pressures if it can group fighting minorities into parties. These cannot jump outside material history, but the contradictions of history cannot be resolved without their own, conscious activity.

Notes

1   K Marx, *A Contribution to the Critique of Political Economy* (London, 1971).
2   K Marx and F Engels, *Collected Works,* vol 6, p166.
3   K Kautsky, *The Economic Doctrines of Karl Marx* (London, 1925), p365.
4   K Kautsky, *Vorläufer der neuren Sozialismus, Erster Band: Kommunistische Bewegungen in Mittelalter* (Berlin 1923), p365. An English translation of part of this work was produced in the 1890s, but is virtually unobtainable today. This is unfortunate, since the weakness in Kautsky's method did not prevent him producing interesting historical studies.
5   K Kautsky, *Ethics and the Materialistic Conception of History* (London, 1906), p81.
6   Like most other mechanical materialists, Kautsky could not stick rigidly to his own method. At points he does suggest that human activity has an important role to play, as when he suggests in his introduction to the *Erfurt Programme* that unless 'society shakes off the burden' of 'the system of private ownership of the means of production' in the way that the 'evolutionary law' decrees, the system will 'pull society down with it into the abyss'. *The Class Struggle* (Chicago, 1910), p87.
7   G Plekhanov, *The Role of the Individual in History,* in *Essays in Historical Materialism* (New York, 1940), p41.
8   Ibid.
9   G Plekhanov, *Fundamental Problems of Marxism* (Moscow, nd), p83.
10   Ibid, p80.
11   *The Role of the Individual in History*, op cit, p44.
12   Which is not at all to blame Plekhanov, who was often quite sophisticated theoretically, for the crudeness of the Stalinist use of his writings.
13   Letter of 25 January, 1894.
14   Letter of 21/22 September, 1890. Cf also his letters to Schmidt of 5 August 1890 and 27 October 1890, and his letter to Mehring of 14 July, 1893.
15   See, for instance, E P Thompson's vigorous polemic against the Althusserians, *The Poverty of Theory* (London, 1978).
16   In *New Left Review*, No 3, May 1960.
17   See *The Poverty of Theory*, op cit, pp251-252.
18   See, for instance, his essay, 'Rethinking Chartism', in *Language of Class* (Cambridge, 1983).
19   See, for instance, Norah Carlin's remark that 'the distinction between base and superstructure is misleading more often than it is useful', in 'Is the Family Part of the Superstructure?', *International Socialism* 26; and Alex Callinicos's suggestion that the Marxist method involves 'starting from relations of production and treating them, not forces of production, as the independent', *Marxism and Philosophy* (London, 1983), p112.
20   G A Cohen, *Karl Marx's Theory of History: a Defence* (Oxford, 1978).
21   See A Labriola, *Essays on the Materialist Conception of History* and *Socialism and Philosophy* (Chicago, 1918).
22   V I Lenin, *Collected Works*, vol 38, p276.
23   See the criticism of Trotsky's position in Isaac Deutscher, *The Prophet Outcast*, pp240-247.
24   *The German Ideology* in Marx and Engels, *Collected Works*, vol 5, pp31 and 41-42. This article was written using an older translation which is marginally different in places from that in the *Collected Works*.
25   Ibid, p31.

26   A Labriola, *Essays on the Materialist Conception of History*, p155.
27   *The German Ideology*, op cit, p31.
28   Ibid, p32.
29   Ibid, p35
30   *Theories of Surplus Value*, part I (Moscow, nd), p280.
31   Quoted earlier.
32   *The Poverty of Philosophy*, op cit, p166.
33   *The Communist Manifesto* in Marx, Engels, Lenin, *The Essential Left* (London 1960), p17.
34   Ibid, p15.
35   For an excellent account of how successive Bronze Age civilisations collapsed into 'dark ages', see V Gordon Childe, *What Happened in History* (Harmondsworth, 1948), pp134, 135-136, 165. For 'regression' in the Amazon, see C Levi Strauss, 'The Concept of Archaism in Anthropology', in *Structural Anthropology* (Harmondsworth, 1968), pp107-112.
36   Cf C Turnbull, *The Mountain People* (London, 1974).
37   *Capital* 1, pp339-340.
38   *The German Ideology*, op cit, p93.
39   This is the point G Lukacs makes in *History and Class Consciousness* (London 1971), pp55-59.
40   See the brief outline of this process in Lindsey German, 'Theories of Patriarchy', *International Socialism*, 12.
41   This is what some patriarchy theorists do, and so does Norah Carlin in 'Is the Family Part of the Superstructure?', *International Socialism*, 26.
42   Norah Carlin gives a lot of attention to these changes, but does not consider where they originate. Her refusal to take the categories of base and superstructure seriously prevents her from doing so.
43   This is the argument of Simon Clarke, 'Althusser's Marxism', in Simon Clarke and others, *One Dimensional Marxism* (London, 1980), p20: 'Social relations of production appear in specific economic, ideological and political forms.'
44   Simon Clarke ends up trying to relate to such contradictions by talking of the 'extent that any social relation is subsumed under the capitalist relations'. The phrasing is much more cumbersome than Marx's own 'base' and 'superstructure', and does not easily enable one to distinguish between the contradictions of the capitalist economy and other elements of contradiction that emerge at points in the concrete history of the system. All conflicts produced by the system are seen as being of equal importance. Politically this leads to a voluntarism very similar to that of post-Althusserianism.
45   Marx and Engels, *The Communist Manifesto* in *Selected Works*, vol 1, (Moscow, 1962), p37.
46   For a much fuller development of these ideas see my *Explaining the Crisis* (London, 1984).
47   *The German Ideology*, op cit, p36.
48   Ibid, p36.
49   Ibid, p43.
50   Ibid, pp43-44.
51   Ibid, p446.
52   Ibid, p183.
53   Marx and Engels, *Collected Works*, vol 5, pp3-5
54   The distinction between different forms of consciousness was one of the fruits of German philosophy and is to be found in the earlier part of Hegel, *Phenomenology of Mind*. Marx, of course, gives a different

significance to this distinction than does Hegel. The problem of how it is possible to move from 'immediate' consciousness to a true general or 'mediated' consciousness is the concern of Lukacs's major philosophical essay, 'Reification and the Consciousness of the Proletariat', in *History and Class Consciousness*, op cit, p446.

55 *The German Ideology*, op cit, p446.
56 Ibid, p449.
57 For a comparison between Marx and Wittgenstein, see A MacIntyre, 'Breaking the Chains of Reason', in E P Thompson (ed), *Out of Apathy*, (London, 1960), p234.
58 I use 'historicist' here in the traditional sense of a relativism which says that there are no general criteria of truth or falsity, but that the correctness of ideas depends on the concrete historical situation in which they are put forward. This is, for instance, the sense in which the term is used by Gramsci. It is not to be confused with Karl Popper's use of it in *The Poverty of Historicism* as a term of abuse to refer to virtually any general account of history.
59 *Theories of Surplus Value* (London, 1951), p202.
60 *Theories of Surplus Value*, vol 1, (Moscow nd), p279.
61 Ibid, p291.
62 *The Eighteenth Brumaire of Louis Bonaparte* in *Collected Works*, vol 11, p103. It is nonsense for post-Althusserians like Gareth Stedman Jones to claim that a Marxist approach involves an attempt to 'decode...political language to read a primal and material expression of interest', *Language of Class*, op cit, p21.
63 A Gramsci, 'Avriamento allo Studio della Filosofia del Materialismo Storico', in *Materialismo Storico* (Turin, 1948), translated in *The Modern Prince* (London, 1957), pp66-67.
64 *Materialismo Storico*, op cit, p38.
65 Ibid, translated in *The Modern Prince*, op cit, p67.
66 As he himself later admitted, V I Lenin, *Collected Works*, vol 6, p491.
67 Note his comment in 1905, 'The working class is instinctively, spontaneously, social democratic...', quoted in C Harman, 'Party and Class', in Tony Cliff and others, *Party and Class* (London, 1996).
68 G Plekhanov, *The Role of the Individual in History*, op cit.
69 L Trotsky, *History of the Russian Revolution* (London 1965), Preface to vol 1, p18.
70 Ibid, Introduction to vols 2 and 3, p510.
71 Ibid, Preface, p18.
72 Ibid, Introduction, p511.
73 Ibid, p19.
74 Ibid, vol 1, p334.
75 Ibid, p302.
76 Ibid, p343.
77 Ibid, p343.
78 Ibid, p339.
79 Ibid, p343.

2

From feudalism to capitalism

The transition from feudalism to capitalism is necessarily of enormous interest to Marxists. It is about how the system we live in rose on the western fringes of Europe and then spread to the rest of the world. It is the most recent example of how one mode of production changes into another, and provided Marx and Engels with many of the insights they incorporated into *The German Ideology* and *The Communist Manifesto*. Arguments about the transition are often, for this reason, as much about the correctness of Marx's and Engels' method as they are about historical fact.

This has been particularly true in the last ten years. A range of people have used the account of the transition to be found in the articles of the American Marxist Robert Brenner—usually quoted as the authority on the question—to attack any notion that the development of the forces of production explains the development of the relations of production and, therefore, of society in general. Brenner's thesis, collected, along with replies from his critics, in T H Ashton and C H E Philpin (eds), *The Brenner Debate*, is the essential starting point for many other writers. So it is that Comninel, in his recent book on interpreting the French Revolution, criticises Marx for falling into 'liberal scientific materialism' when he wrote that:

> The direct relation between the owners of production to the direct producers...always naturally corresponds to a definite stage in the development of the methods of labour and therefore its social productivity.[1]

55

Steve Rigby follows the same path in his *Marxism and History*. He attacks what he calls 'productive force determinism', claiming:

> Marxist historians have been able to make little use of productive force determinism. The transition from feudalism to capitalism, a key test of productive force determinism...[shows]...the redundancy of theories based on it.[2]

Finally, Colin Barker's criticisms of myself in the pages of *International Socialism* for holding 'base' and 'superstructure' to be 'a necessary distinction' rely to a great extent on a view of the transition derived from Brenner.[3] The argument, then, is one that is too important just to be left to those few Marxists who are professional historians.

Two of the most recent books to deal with elements in the transition, although from opposite ends of it, are Jacques Le Goff's *Medieval Civilisation* and Dave McNally's *Political Economy and the Rise of Capitalism*. Le Goff deals with the development of feudalism, from the 6th to the 15th century, from a standpoint which is not Marxist but which is not afraid to borrow insights from Marx. McNally is a Marxist whose study of the way in which political economists in England and France saw society changing in the 17th and 18th centuries is very much influenced by Brenner's arguments.

I hope to show by looking critically at these two books and others that have appeared in the last decade—notably Peter Kriedte's *Peasants, Landlords and Capitalists, Europe and the World Economy 1500-1800* and *Industrialisation before Industrialisation*—that Marx's account of the interrelation between the development of the forces and relations of production can be used to explain the transition, indeed, that it is the only account that provides such an explanation.[4]

The scope of the transition

Before the argument can begin it is necessary to spell out what the 'transition' was about. There has been a tendency in the recent discussions among Marxists to see it in terms of the change from the organisation of society (or at least of the economy) of the 14th century to that of the late 18th century.[5] But the scale of the 'transition' is best grasped by comparing feudalism in its 'classic' form, that of the 10th century, with capitalism in its classic form, that of the late 19th and early 20th centuries.

Tenth century feudalism was an overwhelmingly rural society. Almost the whole of the population lived off the land, in more or less self contained manorial villages. Control of each manor lay with the feudal lord—either a warrior or an ecclesiastical body—exercising political and juridical as well as economic power in the locality. The mass of peasants were serfs unable to leave the manor where they tilled strips of land for themselves but also provided for the livelihood of the feudal lord, either by forced labour on his estate ('demesne') or by payment of rent in kind. Money played very little role in rural life, with the feudal lords using serf labour to produce non-agricultural produce in demesne workshops.

Towns were few, far between and small, with many town dwellers themselves tilling plots for part of their livelihood. Trade was carried out by despised travelling peddlers who provided those few essential goods (for instance, salt) which the local serfs could not produce. Because land was the only source of substantial wealth, control of it was the motive force behind the behaviour of the ruling class—and the cause of repeated armed conflicts within it.

The feudal lord exploited the peasants, often forcing them into abject poverty. Yet he could not exploit in order to amass profits. The aim of production was consumption (including conspicuous consumption), not accumulation. As Marx put it, 'The limits to the exploitation of the feudal serf were determined by the walls of the stomach of the feudal lord.'

Contrast capitalism at its height. Urban life dominates, so that even owners of agricultural land are based in towns. The great majority of the population work in industry or 'services'. Money plays an absolutely central role. Everyone depends on selling something in order to get the means of livelihood—even if all most people have to sell is their labour power. Most importantly, there is no limit to the accumulation of wealth. Everything can be turned into money and members of the ruling class can own endless amounts of money. What drives the system forward is not the consumption of the ruling class, but what Marx called self expansion of capital, the endless pursuit of accumulation for the sake of accumulation.

The differences between 10th century feudalism and modern

capitalism are not, of course, just economic. The economic transformation has been accompanied by enormous change in
attitudes, in what are sometimes called 'mentalities' or 'spiritu-
alities'. In classic feudalism everyone was born into a fixed
hierarchy of ranks (even if a few people did manage to climb
from one to another). The great majority of people never moved
more than a few miles (on average about five) from their birth-
place, and their knowledge of the world was very much restricted
to this locality. They spoke a local dialect, virtually incomprehensible to someone living only 40 or 50 miles away. They had
virtually no conception of the world as it was before they were
born. There was no notion of the nation. The state was whoever
exercised physical power over you at a given point in time—
and that could change very rapidly. Everyone assumed things
would be done more or less as they had been done by parents and
grandparents.

Again things could not be more different under capitalism.
Everyone, at least in theory, has equal political and judicial rights
with everyone else. Everyone is born into a nation and speaks a
language spoken by millions or even hundreds of millions of
other people. Everyone assumes life will be very different for
them from what it was for parents and grandparents.

Explanations for the transition

There are two main sorts of theories of the transition. First there
are those which see it as following from the growth of trade, of
a powerful class of merchants, and of towns as the centre of both.
The best known version of this theory is that developed by the
Belgian economic historian, Enri Pirenne. He claimed that feudalism arose as Europe's Mediterranean trade was disrupted by
the rise of Islam. This led to European society turning in on itself.
As long distance trade virtually ceased, the towns, as the trading
centres, declined, and money lost its role. The ruling class
became dependent for its consumption upon production in virtually autarchic manors because of the lack of alternatives:

> All classes of the population from the Emperor, who had no other
> revenues than those derived from his landed property, down to the
> humblest serf lived directly or indirectly on the produce of the
> soil, whether they raised them by their own labour, or confined

themselves to collecting and consuming them. Moveable wealth no longer played any part in economic life—All social existence was founded on property or the possession of land...[6]

But from the 11th century onwards a new growth of trade began around the edges of Europe from Byzantium and Venice in the south, and from the Baltic coasts in the north. The crusades drove the Muslims from strategic points in the Mediterranean so that it was 'opened, or rather re-opened, to western navigation. As in the time of Rome, communications were established from one end to the other... The exploitation of its waters by Islam was at an end'.[7]

The revival of maritime commerce was accompanied by its rapid penetration inland. Not only was agriculture stimulated by the demand for its produce and the exchange economy of which it now became part, but a new export industry was born.[8]

What happened in the Mediterranean was matched in the north as Scandinavian trade brought the countries bordering the North Sea into contact with those bordering the Baltic and gave a stimulus to the growth of towns like Ghent, Bruges, Lille and London. Soon, too, rivers like the Rhine and the Rhone were being used to link the commerce of northern Europe and the commerce of the Mediterranean—and in the process this gave a forward push to towns and cities in between.

These changes led to the transformation of the humble and despised peddlers of the 9th century into the powerful merchant class of the 13th and 14th centuries. This class was protected from the feudal lords by the fortifications of its towns and adopted a new set of attitudes based upon endless profit making.

A range of thinkers have held a similar view to Pirenne, stressing the external impetus of the growth of export trade as leading to an internal transformation of European feudalism. Paul Sweezy, for instance, writes:

Long distance trade could be a creative force bringing into existence a system of production for exchange alongside the old feudal system of production for use.[9]

Immanuel Wallerstein puts the decisive change a couple of centuries later than Pirenne and Sweezy, stressing the importance of the conquest of American colonies in the transition. 'Europe's upper strata', he argues, responded to a crisis of feudal society in the 15th century by overseas expansion and the creation of colonies and politically dependent zones with which trade could take place on the basis of 'unequal exchange', transferring surplus products from 'the periphery' to 'the core' of the system.[10] The equation of capitalism with profits from trade is also to be found in the work of the non-Marxist economic historian Fernand Braudel,[11] and in some of the writings of the sociologist Max Weber.[12]

What can be called the Pirenne-Sweezy-Wallerstein view has one great strength. It focuses on the contrast between production for use, characteristic of pre-capitalist societies, and production simply in order to expand exchange value. As Wallerstein puts it, what characterised capitalism was that:

> Capital…came to be used with the primary object or intent of self expansion. In this system past accumulations were capital only to the extent that they were used to accumulate more of the same… It was this relentless and curiously self disregarding goal of the holder of capital, the accumulation of still more capital…which we denominate as capitalist…[13]

But there are problems with such accounts of the rise of capitalism which other theorists have been quick to focus on:
i) It doesn't explain the patterns of trade it points to. Pirenne, for instance, simply asserts that the new Islamic states on the eastern and southern shores of the Mediterranean could not trade with Christian western Europe in the 7th to 10th centuries—even though he recognises that they continued to trade with Christian Byzantium and its dependency Venice.[14]

Wallerstein has no explanation as to how it was that Europe was able to seize control of other parts of the world and impose 'unequal exchange' on them, given that he insists Europe was, 'in terms of the forces of production, the cohesion of its historical system and its relative state of human knowledge', more backward than some other parts of the world, even if not as 'primitive' as others.[15]

ii) The great merchants of the medieval period might have originated from backgrounds quite different to those of the feudal ruling class and might have adopted different attitudes at first. But they tended very quickly to forget those differences and to join with that ruling class, using the profits from trade to buy manors. Braudel suggests that families rarely remained in trade for more than three generations before buying their way into the old ruling class. This was what happened to the great German merchant family the Fuggers, and to the most powerful families in the Italian city states by the 16th century. Even where wealthy merchants remained in trade they soon put the stress on establishing ties with the old ruling class in order to establish monopoly control over their line of business, rather than on revolutionary subversion of that class.

Far from pushing for a new system of production in opposition to feudalism, the wealthiest merchants often became conservative forces defending the status quo.

iii) Those involved in the handicraft trades of the towns could be just as conservative. The rights which the towns obtained for themselves in the 'interstices' of the feudal order were often used to establish guild organisations of trades which sought, not to transform old methods of production, but to preserve them against competition from newcomers. In this way they aspired to guarantee the guild members an assured livelihood, even if this meant holding back the growth of the towns.[16]

iv) Merchants might have been involved in making money for the sake of making money—the self expansion of capital. But they had not developed a way of doing this systematically over a long period of time. This was only possible if they established a new organisation of production, capable of continually expanding the surplus obtained from the labour force. This could not happen so long as agriculture was cramped by feudal relations of production and industry by guild regulation. The merchants could buy in order to sell, and so expand their wealth—in the notation used by Marx, they could go through the cycle $M\text{-}C\text{-}M'$. But they did not control an intermediate stage of production and exploitation, that is $M\text{-}C\text{-}[P]\text{-}C'\text{-}M'$.

This meant the long term possibilities for any individual merchant family were very limited. It could take advantage of existing discrepancies in prices between different countries or regions (eg for spices from the east or grain from Poland), but could not find a mechanism for systematically creating such a discrepancy. Then those gains could easily be wiped out—by competition from rival merchants raising buying prices and cutting selling prices, by the accidental loss of a ship at sea or by the looting which was an inevitable accompaniment of feudal wars.

This could not change until forms of production came into being based upon wage labour. As Marx put it:

> Value, the objectified labour which exists in the form of money, could only grow by exchange with a commodity whose use value itself consisted in the ability to increase exchange value... But such use value is only possessed by living labour capacity...
>
> Value, money, can therefore only be transformed into capital through exchange with living labour capacity.[17]

This cannot happen unless workers are both able and willing to sell their labour power—able because it does not belong to slave owners, willing because there is no other way they can turn it into the commodities they need in order to subsist. Again, as Marx puts it:

> Money can, in general, be transformed into capital, or the money owners turned into capitalists, only to the extent that the free worker is available on the commodity market: free in so far as he, on the one hand, has at his disposal his own labour capacity as a commodity, and on the other hand has no other commodity at his disposal, is free, completely rid of, all the objective conditions for the realisation of his labour capacity...and therefore, as a mere subject, a mere personification of his own labour capacity, is a worker in the same sense that the money owner is a capitalist, as subject and repository of objectified labour...[18]

But this condition is not brought about just by an increase in external market pressures on a pre-capitalist society. In fact, the growth of markets in the 16th, 17th and 18th centuries did not just lead to the rise of capitalist production based on wage labour in places like Britain and the low countries; it also led to the growth of plantation based slave labour in the Caribbean and the American South, and to a renewed growth of feudalism in much of eastern Europe.[19]

The arguments of Dobb

The inadequacies of the Pirenne-Sweezy-Wallerstein view have led to a different range of theories which stress the growth of capitalist production within feudalism between the 15th and 18th centuries. Maurice Dobb's *Studies in the Development of Capitalism*, first published in 1946, argued that the breakdown of feudalism and the development of capitalism had to be understood in terms of factors internal to the western European societies, not to external trade.

He dealt at length with the growth of merchant capital and, alongside it and often subordinated to it, of handicraft production in both the towns and the countryside. But he concluded that the merchants were too much part of feudal society to have played a central role in its transformation. The key to this transformation lay within the old mode of production itself. As he later put it: 'What I am asserting is [that] the growth of trade exercised its influence to the extent that it accentuated the internal conflicts within the old mode of production'.[20] The central conflict within feudalism Dobb saw as being between 'the petty producers' and the feudal exploiting class:

> No one is suggesting that the class struggle of peasants against lords gives rise, in any direct and simple way, to capitalism. What this does is to modify the dependence of the petty mode of production upon feudal overlordship and eventually to shake loose the small producer from feudal exploitation.[21]

> [In England] by the end of the 15th century the feudal order had disintegrated and grown weaker in a number of ways. The peasant revolt of the previous century, it is true, had been suppressed. But it had left its ghost to haunt the old order in the form of the standing threat of a peasant flight from the manor into the woods or hills or to swell the growing number of day labourers and artisans in the towns. The ranks of the old nobility were thinned and divided; the smaller estates lacking sufficient labour-services had taken to leasing or to wage labour... Merchants were buying land, estates were being mortgaged and a kulak class of improving peasant farmers were becoming serious competitors in local markets and as rural employers of labour.[22]

The old feudal ruling class survived these changes in so far as it was left in control of the state and of a substantial portion of society's income. But it was decisively weakened by them, a full two centuries before the capitalist mode of production had established itself:

> Between the 14th and the end of the 16th [centuries]...the petty mode of production was in the process of emancipating itself from feudal exploitation, but was not yet subjected (at least not to any

63

significant degree) to capitalist relations of production which were eventually to destroy it.[23]

The capitalism which finally developed was different to the merchant capitalism of the medieval towns: 'We cannot date the dawn of this system from the first signs of large scale trading and of a merchant class... We must look for when changes in the mode of production occur, in the sense of a direct subordination of the producer to the capitalist'.[24] This Dobb does not see as happening until the second half of the 16th century:

> The 200 year period which separated Edward III and Elizabeth was certainly transitional in character. A merchant bourgeoisie had grown in wealth and influence... [I]t stood in a position of co-partner rather than antagonist to the nobility and in Tudor times partly merged with it. Its appearance exercised little direct effect on the mode of production... In the urban handicrafts and the rise of the well to do and middling well to do freehold farmers one sees a mode of production which had won its independence from feudalism: petty production of the worker owner artisan or peasant type...[25]

There are two main problems with Dobb's argument. First, he insists that the collapse of feudalism must be mainly due to internal factors. But he does not specify what they are, apart from his references to peasant revolts and a crisis among the nobility. He does not connect either of these to the development of productive forces within feudalism.

In *Studies* he depicted these as virtually stagnant, arguing that 'it was the inefficiency of feudalism as a system of production, coupled with the growing needs of the ruling class for revenue, that was primarily responsible for its decline',[26] and that where a growth in output did occur under feudalism, it was a result of an increased labour force taking new lands into cultivation.[27]

In his debate with Sweezy (written in 1950) he recognised that 'the feudal period witnessed considerable changes in technique and the later centuries of feudalism showed marked differences from those of early feudalism'.[28] But he does not draw any connection between such changes and the crisis of feudalism, and can still, in the same piece, simply refer to feudal methods of production as 'relatively primitive'.[29] This led him to a second problem—that of the two century period between the collapse of feudalism and the

rise of capitalism in which a mode of production not to be identified with either predominated. Marx recognised that there was such
a transition period, but insisted, 'the economic structure of capitalist society grows out of the economic structure of feudal society.
The dissolution of one sets free the elements of the other'.[30] Dobb,
by contrast, stresses the gap between the collapse of feudalism and
the rise of capitalism.

This, of course, did not prove Dobb wrong. Marx was only
human and could easily make mistaken judgments. However,
Dobb's own position raised all sorts of awkward questions as to
the nature of the ruling class in that period—as Sweezy and
others pointed out in the debate in the 1950s. Dobb was only able
to answer such questions by saying it must have been 'feudal'
otherwise the English Revolution of the 1640s cannot have been
a bourgeois revolution. He may have been able to get away with
that sort of argument in the 1950s, when those in Moscow
presided over a Stalinised caricature of Marxism and could pass
decrees on what was and what was not to be regarded as a bourgeois revolution. But today the most likely response to the
argument would be, 'OK, the English Revolution had nothing to
do with the rise of the bourgeoisie.'

However much Dobb twisted and turned in presenting his
case, he could not avoid interposing a huge gap between the
decline of one mode of production and the rise of another, which
makes it seem as if the two were not connected and were both
historical accidents.

Brenner's arguments

The debate of the 1950s resumed in the mid-1970s with the pub-
lication of two articles by Robert Brenner. One was an onslaught
on the Pirenne-Sweezy-Wallerstein position and appeared in *New
Left Review*.[31] The other, in the academic journal *Past and Present*,
concentrated its fire on attempts by non-Marxist economic historians such as Postan and Hatcher to explain the crisis of feudalism
through the impact of a rising population upon limited food
resources—a theory Brenner describes as 'neo-Malthusian'.[32]
Both articles put forward the same argument, although from
different angles.

What Brenner does, essentially, is to take up Dobb's argument,
but simplify it in a way which gives it greater polemical power.

To this end he takes up and expands just one of the elements Dobb sees at work in this period, the leasing of estates by former feudal lords to farmers who employ wage labour. He ignores the mass of other material which exists in Dobb's *Studies*—on merchant capital, handicraft production, rural and urban manufacturing, the putting out system, and the class struggle in towns.

Brenner gives added emphasis to Dobb's argument that it is the struggle between agricultural exploiters and agricultural producers which brings about a great crisis of feudal relations of production in the 14th century. But he then goes further than Dobb and insists that it was on the land that capitalism was born in the following period—again as a result of the balance of forces between the two great landed classes of feudalism, the lords and the peasants. Capitalism emerges, for him, neither as merchant capitalism nor as industrial capitalism but as agrarian capitalism:

> It was, indeed, in the last analysis an agricultural revolution based on the emergence of capitalist class relations in the countryside which made it possible for England to become the first nation to experience industrialisation.[33]

This could only happen because of the outcome of the class struggle under feudalism:

> The original breakthrough in Europe to a system of more or less sustaining growth was dependent upon a two sided development of class relations: first the breakdown of systems of lordly surplus extraction by means of extra-economic compulsion, second the undermining of peasant possession or the abating of any trend towards full peasant ownership of the land.[34]

Agrarian capitalism involves the ex-feudal lord, faced with a shortage of cash needed to meet the requirements of military conflict with other feudal lords,[35] renting out land to big peasants who in turn employ wage labour. The lord will then have an interest in improving the productivity of the land, so as to raise the rents he can demand (transforming traditional feudal rents into market determined capitalist rent). And the big peasant will seek to exploit those poor peasants who have been forced to sell their labour power to him, in as efficient a manner as possible—to determine his levels of productivity and production in relation to the demands of endless accumulation, not of consumption.

But before this can happen control over the land has to develop in two ways. First, the peasants have to rebel on such a scale as to free themselves from the main burden of feudal services and dues. This prevents the lords from using unpaid labour to till demesne land and so raise their incomes (as happened in eastern Europe). Second, the lords have to retain enough power to prevent peasants getting control of land themselves and tilling it as independent small proprietors (as happened in France, according to Brenner).

Brenner claims that his account roots the transition from feudalism to capitalism in production and in the class struggle, while the account of Sweezy and Wallerstein does not and is 'neo-Smithian' rather than Marxist. But there are as many problems with his explanation as with theirs:

i) It rests upon the unsatisfactory notion that the future society is determined by the struggle between the lord and an undifferentiated peasantry in the countryside. For him there has to be an intermediate outcome to this class struggle. If the peasants win everything, as he claims happened in France, then capitalism does not develop. Likewise, if the lords win everything, as in eastern Europe, it does not develop either. What is required is what Brenner says happened in England—the lords lose some of their power, but not all of it.[36] History, it seems, is made by those exploited classes who fight but don't fight to the end.

Now, of course, there are situations in which the outcome of historical events is completely different to the intention of those who take part in them. But was this true of all of those engaged in the great social and political struggles of the transition period? Or did not some at least of the leading participants feel that they were fighting for a new form of society, a form which had certain features we could identify as capitalist?

If the poor peasants in Britain were only half victorious, might this not be connected with the influence on them of other social classes who were already setting themselves goals which pointed to a society based upon capitalist forms of exploitation—even if they described these goals in religious terms?

Brenner's formulations imply a complete separation between the ideological objectives of the social forces involved in conflicts and the outcome of these conflicts. But this makes it very difficult to see what connection there is between the transition from feudalism to capitalism and the huge social, political and ideological conflicts of the period. People rarely enter into battle with the goal of only half winning, yet according to Brenner's arguments only those who did so could advance society. So it is that wars, revolutions and civil wars (as opposed to peasant rebellions) have no place in Brenner's account of the period. Nor do the huge changes in human attitudes associated with the Renaissance, Reformation and Enlightenment. It seems simply a great coincidence that the centuries of the transition were also centuries which saw huge revolutionary upheavals. It is hardly surprising that his account has led one of his disciples, Comninel, to accept the argument of 'revisionist' historians that the English and French revolutions had nothing to do with the rise of the bourgeoisie.

Brenner claims his account puts class struggle at the centre of the transition in a way that other accounts do not. But his is a very narrow view of class struggle, restricted to the immediate struggle at the point of production between peasants and feudal lords and excluding any reference to the global social changes which one or other class would like, in however confused a way, to bring about. Accounts of the class struggle under capitalism in these terms are usually described as 'economism' and the apolitical methods of struggle based on them as 'syndicalism'. Brenner has transmitted this notion of the class struggle back into the rural class struggle of the late medieval period. His approach has been described by critics and supporters alike as 'political' Marxism;[37] it would be more accurate to say he has given birth to a sort of rustic economism.[38]

ii) Brenner does not even try to explain why this intermediate outcome to the class struggle should occur after the crisis of feudalism in the 14th century, but not earlier. The struggle between the exploited and the exploiting rural classes was, for him, a constant feature of feudalism. So why did not previous demographic crises—for instance that at the time of the collapse of Charlemagne's empire—lead to a transition? Indeed, on his reasoning it is difficult to see why the collapse of the Roman Empire should have led to feudalism and not to 'agrarian capitalism'. For he never even attempts to locate any dynamic in feudalism which could account for differences between one period and another.

iii) Separating the direct agricultural producers from control over the means of production does not produce a drive towards the self expansion of capitalism on its own. There is no reason why it should not simply lead to the landowners using hired labour to provide for their own consumption.[39] The only thing which rules out this sort of production for use on the basis of hired labour is the existence of the market and commodity production. Brenner takes this for granted when he writes of the improving landlords and their tenants producing crops for cash, but does not explain where this market came from.

iv) Brenner's account simply ignores the role of towns. For him the classes based in the towns seem to play a thoroughly reactionary role.

> The essence of the urban economy based on luxury production for a limited market was economic restriction—and in particular control over the labour market.[40]

The urban artisans could be anti-aristocratic, but were just as frightened of labour market competition from a free peasantry as they were of the feudal lords. And:

> The urban patriciate would tend to align themselves with the nobility against the peasantry. Both these classes had a common interest in maintaining social order and the defence of property and in protecting their mutually beneficial relationships of commercial exchange.[41]

He claims that examples show that 'the towns rarely aided peasant resistance to serfdom, nor was the success of such resistance apparently dependent on such aid'.[42] He dismisses the old argument that the towns presented a way of escape from serfdom for the rural peasants, on the grounds that the towns never accounted for more than 10 percent of the population.

Yet there is a mass of empirical material which at least partially contradicts his argument. Capitalist economic development in the countryside would have been impossible if urban based classes had not existed to buy the products of agriculture. This buying did not simply occur. It was encouraged by the merchants, however much they might have politically accepted feudalism. F J Fisher long ago pointed to the role of London based merchants in encouraging the development of the English countryside:

> During the century before 1650 London was large enough to exercise a great influence upon the agriculture of the surrounding counties causing a rapid spread of market gardening, increasing

local specialisation and encouraging the wholesalers to move back
up the chain of production and exchange to engage directly in
the production of food or to sink capital in the improvement of
agricultural facilities.[43]

Poulterers made loans to warreners and themselves bred poultry.
Fruiterers helped to establish orchards and leased them when
established. Butchers themselves became graziers.[44]

It has often been pointed out that individual peasant families
living on the verge of subsistence bought very little from the
towns or from itinerant traders. But they did buy some essential
things (for example, salt, the small amounts of iron used in their
ploughs, leather for horse harnesses, occasionally the cheapest
sorts of cloth, the services of blacksmiths).[45] Sylvia Thrupp has
gone so far as to state: 'The popular notion that peasants bought
only farm tools and salt, relying on their wives to make everything else, is…no longer tenable', pointing to evidence from late
11th century documents of local trade in 'feathers, wool, tables,
bedrolls, skins of cats, lambs, wedding outfits, rings, knives and
harnesses'.[46] Georges Duby has noted that: 'A widespread pop-
ularisation of aristocratic usage reached even into the peasant
world by the 14th century'.[47] And, of course, the richer peasants
who did develop in the direction of capitalist farming were much
more dependent on industrial products and market networks run
by urban based merchants than the average.

At a minimum, the towns—and not just the large cities, but the
many smaller towns[48]—provided a market for the output of the
improving farmers and some of the inputs that made improvement possible. These inputs were not necessarily just physical:
also of importance was the spread of knowledge about how
improvement was possible. One contributing factor to the economic advance of Bohemia in the century before the Thirty Years
War was the circulation of books detailing the most productive
agricultural methods: 'Printers disseminated…technical books,
especially in the sphere of agriculture'.[49]

Le Goff writes, with reference to the period which Brenner sees
as the taking off point of 'agrarian capitalism' in England: 'A network of [small towns] set up a kind of fine weft under the
stretched and loosened warp of a population decimated by the
plague and thinly scattered because of deserted villages'.[50] It was
this 'fine weft' that enabled production for the market to penetrate

into the countryside and the separation of direct producers from the means of production to lead to the self expansion of value.

There were certainly some occasions on which the towns did loosen the hold of the feudal lords over the serfs. Le Goff, for instance, points out that:

> The town could force rural lords to free their serfs as happened on a large scale in 13th century Italy, at Vercelli in 1243, Bologna in 1256-7 and Florence in 1289.[51]

The famous Peasant Revolt of 14th century England did not just involve peasants, but also urban journeymen, even if the London oligarchy helped to crush it.

For some peasants at least, flight to the town was a way of escaping serfdom: hence the well known German saying, '*Stadtluft macht frei*' (the town air makes you free). Hence too the clashes which could occur between small English towns and the feudal lords who had first established them.[52]

As for Brenner's claim that the towns contained too small a proportion of the population to influence what happened on the land, this begs the question of what happened when the towns grew bigger. And this happened in the two countries which did make the breakthrough to capitalism: in 1650 in Holland 8 percent of the total population lived in Amsterdam alone, and in England 7 percent lived in London, while, in France only 2.5 percent lived in Paris.[53] One estimate suggests that in the century after 1650 one in seven of England's population lived in London at some point in their life.[54] It is a strange coincidence that the towns should have this influence precisely where the chains of feudalism were successfully smashed, while in the countries of eastern Europe, where the towns were much smaller and more dispersed, feudal relations could strengthen their grip over agriculture.

Again Brenner's picture of all the urban classes cohabiting peacefully with the feudal lords hardly fits with the facts. For the towns were centres of ideological ferment within feudal society.

In the late 12th and 13th centuries the growth of new religious orders based in the town—one founded by a Lyons merchant, Peter Waldes, another by the son of an Assisi merchant, Francis—were seen by the church as a dangerous ideological threat. Le Goff tells how the heretical movement of the late 13th century 'joined together heterogeneous coalitions of social groups, in which sections of the nobility, of the new burgess class, and of the artisan class, combined…' in which 'men' displayed 'an attitude of complete rejection' of 'the world, with its social organisation (feudal society) and its guide, the Church of Rome…'[55]

Two hundred and fifty years later the Protestant ideas which were to plunge Europe into a century of religious wars and revolutions were disseminated from towns. And in the great revolution of 1789-94 the intervention of the urban sans culottes was of major importance in providing a central, national, political focus for the bitter class struggle waged in the countryside. The towns may, on average, have made up only a tenth of the population, but this tenth was decisive as the focal point for agitation and propaganda in opposition to the old feudal attitudes. An account of the transition from feudalism to capitalism which does not, as a minimum, integrate the role of the towns cannot be an adequate account.

v) Brenner more or less ignores the changes taking place in production techniques, both in town and countryside, in the centuries before the transition. Amongst these were the advances in printing and papermaking, the development of mechanical clocks, advances in textile manufacture, the development of guns and gunpowder, and the advances in shipbuilding and navigation that made sea trade with the East Indies and the conquest of the Americas possible.

Brenner writes:

> The feudal socio-property system established certain distinctive mechanisms for distributing income…which led to economic stagnation and involution.
>
> It…imposed upon the members of the major social classes strategies for reproducing themselves which when applied on an economy wide basis were incompatible with the requirements of growth.[56]

Yet, as we shall see, the feudal period saw quite considerable economic advance.

vi) Brenner makes no attempt to integrate the development of agriculture with the development of industry. In fact, in the 16th century, for him a century of rising 'agrarian' capitalism in Britain, the majority of woollen exports were manufactured exports. By the end of the 17th century, although not more than

20 or 30 percent of England's population was outside agriculture, 44 percent of national income was non-agricultural and textiles accounted for 70 percent of exports. As one history of the industry tells, 'By the beginning of the 17th century the western cloth industry had long been a field in which large capitals had been employed... The large capitalists dominated the industry, [even if] the small clothiers formed a large element in it'.[57] At least one maker of white cloth claimed to employ nearly 1,000 persons.[58] It is rather bizarre to call a society in which such things occurred agrarian capitalism!

Brenner can write, 'Quite possibly the spectacular rise of the English cloth production for export from the late 15th century was what set off the overall process of English economic development...'[59] and of 'the unique symbiotic relationship between agriculture and industry'[60] in England. But he makes no attempt to investigate the impact of industry on agriculture.

The rival theories: the unity of opposites

Both sets of theories have something in common. They both try to explain the transition without talking about the development of the forces of production under feudalism. The Pirenne-Wallerstein-Sweezy position sees change as being external to the feudal system. Brenner claims to disagree with this. But in his analysis the only thing he is concerned to study in the feudal system is 'the class structure'. The way in which this changes under the impact of the great social classes is, for him, the factor which explains the transformation of society as a whole. There is little or no room in his account of social change for giving any causative role to the development of the forces of production.[61] What matters to him is class struggle, and he shows little concern with changes in the material setting within which it takes place, except in so far as demographic developments lead to shortages of foodstuffs and increased struggle between classes.[62]

Sweezy, Wallerstein and Brenner all claim to be Marxists. Yet Marx's own version of historical materialism was based on the claim that to understand the development of any mode of production you have to look at the interrelation between the development of the forces of production and the relations of production. Changes in the forces of production lead to small scale

73

cumulative changes in the relations between people which, eventually, throw into question the whole organisation of society.[63]

This is as true of feudalism as of any stage in the history of human society. Feudalism is a very slowly changing form of society. But it is not a static one. Sylvia Thrupp suggests that 'the best medieval rates of general economic growth, if they could be counted by decades to balance the effects of good and bad harvests, would come to perhaps half of one percent'.[64] This is very slow by capitalist standards. But it still implies that massive advances occurred over 500 or 1,000 years. Estimates of population growth point to the scale of the change. The medieval period saw four great demographic crises. Three of these, in the sixth, 13th and 17th centuries, were associated with famines and plagues and led to cuts in the total population of up to 50 percent (the other one, in the 9th century, seems to have been less acute and only to have brought to an end a period of population growth).[65]

Yet the total population at the end of this 1,000 year period was much higher than at beginning. It was three times larger after the plague of the 14th century than it was after the plague of the sixth century. Or, to put it another way, the number of people in Europe at the dawn of the Renaissance was more than twice that at the peak of Roman civilisation.

The period from the 10th to the 13th century in particular saw considerable economic growth. This is a key part of the Pirenne argument and is accepted by Brenner. But the Pirenne school locates this growth simply as a response to external market stimuli, and Brenner sees it as based simply on the clearing of new land on which old agricultural techniques were applied—'quantitative economic growth' was possible for peasant based production, but 'it could not sustain a qualitative breakthrough into economic development'.[66]

Yet historical research in the last two or three decades has shown that there were considerable advances in the forces of production during the feudal period, both in industry and agriculture. As Lynn White has pointed out:

> The growth of technology is the least developed and most rapidly shifting part of economic history... The state of records and the tastes of historians have combined to distort past activities. Today our view is being somewhat rectified by a surge of interest in

studying, with what evidence is available, improved methods of production and transportation, the emergence of new types of goods, and changing ways of living and thinking...[67]

Expansion rooted in the feudal mode of production

The view that feudalism was a stagnant mode of production is linked to another contention that has become almost a commonplace among many Marxists: that because it was based on extra-economic coercion rather than the 'economic' interaction between buyers and sellers of labour power to be found under capitalism, it had no economic roots.[68] But, as Marx and Engels always pointed out (read, for instance, Engels' *The Role of Violence in History*)[69], the ability of one class to coerce another class itself depends on prior economic developments, on the development of the forces of production. Feudalism arose in the first place because it could maintain and develop production at a time when the preceding mode of production was in terminal crisis.

The slave society of ancient antiquity which dominated the Mediterranean area until the 4th and 5th century AD collapsed through its inability to develop the forces of production after the second century. The wealth of the Roman Empire was created by slavery[70] and the ruling class of the empire sought to increase its wealth through increasing the number of slaves, to be obtained by warfare, rather than by any concern with increasing the productivity of labour.

> Rome exploited its empire without creating anything. No technical innovation had occurred since the Hellenistic age. Rome's empire was fed by pillage. Successful wars provided slave manpower and precious metals drawn from the hoarded treasures of the East.[71]

On this basis it was able to build a civilisation centred on a series of great towns, where the ruling class that exploited the countryside resided. But a point was eventually reached, as early as the second half of the 2nd century, where the source of the surplus for maintaining this urban civilisation began to run out: the supply of slaves began to decrease. Incessant wars could more or less hold the boundaries of the empire for some two or three centuries more, but they could not overcome the economic stagnation—and with it the proliferation of famines, plagues, intra-ruling class civil wars and, on occasions, revolts from below. Finally the empire as a whole collapsed in the face of 'barbarian' tribes, initially invited into its boundaries in a desperate attempt to fight off other barbarian tribes. The whole superstructure of urban civilisation came crashing down, as the 'base' of slave based production ceased to be adequate to support it.

But even while the old mode of production was falling apart, a new one was emerging to supplant it. It did so in two ways. First, it emerged within the boundaries of the empire itself as a way of preserving production and exploitation. A section of the ruling class discovered that they could protect themselves from the collapse of the economy of the empire as a whole by granting land to former slaves or former soldiers in return for produce in kind and/or labour services.

Meanwhile, a similar structure of exploitation was also arising out of intrinsic developments in the Germanic tribes which settled in the lands in and around the old empire. Formerly free peasants often found that the only way they could get military protection from marauding bands (whether 'barbarian' or Roman) was to accept a similar serf type arrangement with a powerful local lord. It was military strength, violence, which enabled the new feudal exploiters to protect holdings from armed raiders and to force the exploited class to accept the status of serfdom. But military strength in turn depended on the fact that the new system of exploitation enabled local, more or less self contained, economic units to survive the disintegration of the old mode of production, and not just survive—the new arrangement was soon more productive than the old.

The new serf peasant was necessarily more attentive to his own plot of land than the slave had been to his master's. And the new feudal lord had to pay some heed to the needs of peasant based production. It was the only source by which he could seek to protect his living standards in the midst of the collapse of the old slave economy and protect himself from marauding warrior bands.

Kriedte quite rightly notes that:

The logic of the manorial system based on serf labour demanded that the lord had to preserve the peasant holding at all costs because of its role as a supplier of labour power and draft power. Therefore he had to assist peasants in emergencies which arose from harvest failures and other causes.[72]

It was not only a question of preserving existing levels of production. In the early feudal period the 'walls of the feudal lord's stomach' were by no means full. His diet, though more plentiful, was hardly more varied than that of the serfs: he lived on bread, meat and, in northern climes, ale. He clothed himself in rough and uncomfortable peasant spun garments. He lived in a cold and draughty rough built castle. In such circumstances he had every incentive to encourage the planting of new crops and increases in output which could be exchanged for specialised luxury goods to be obtained from outside the manor. Duby tells how: 'The [lord's] steward, anxious never to find himself in short supply, naturally tried to increase output, especially of corn'.[73] There was 'no wish to accumulate goods', but he always wanted 'to have something in hand to provide for the "family".'[74]

Le Goff notes:

From the moment when the ruling class established itself in the countryside and became a class of great landowners, the landed aristocracy encouraged progress in agricultural production. Not that the aristocracy took a direct interest in managing its estates although some ecclesiastical lords and high Carolingian functionaries did so, but the dues and services which it extracted from the peasant masses must have stimulated the latter to improve their methods of cultivation to some extent to pay the dues...[75]

Precisely because all the wealth of the feudal lord came from land, he could develop an interest in building up productivity— in encouraging 'his' serfs to use new techniques of production (often, in fact, old techniques known during antiquity but not used because they did not fit in with slave production). Of course, many feudal lords did not behave in this way. They were prepared to push their serfs below the subsistence level as they squandered their output or devoted it solely to military adventures against other feudal lords. But at the end of the day, the most effective feudal lords, even when it came simply to military adventures, had to be those who maintained an adequate material base from which to operate. And that meant some concern with maintaining and improving serf productivity.

So after the 'invasions' of the 10th century:

> Once the barbarian tribes had settled, the new masters were forced
> to form a real policy of land development. The history of the ear-
> liest dukes of Normandy, written by the canon Dubdo of St
> Quentin in the 11th century, shows how the Normans, during the
> first century after they had installed themselves in Normandy,
> turned themselves into cultivators under the leadership of the
> dukes, who put farming tools made of iron, especially ploughs,
> under their protection.[76]

Far from being concerned solely with violence, it was individual feudal lords who organised and financed the colonisation
of new lands throughout the feudal period. Again, the feudal lords
were the driving force in the spread of the first, and for a long time
most important, form of mechanisation, the water mill. The feudal
lord wanted it built so as to force the peasants to use it and release
more surplus for himself (usually obtained by making peasants
hand over dues for the use of contrivances which had, in the last
resort, been produced out of their labour); the fact of the well documented resistance of serfs to the water mill—they preferred to
keep the dues themselves and use the old hand mill—does not dis-
prove the point at all. Indeed, it shows that even the violence of
feudal lords could, on occasion, raise general productivity.

The abbots and monks who collectively exploited the peasants
in those manors in ecclesiastical hands were the only literate
group in early medieval society. As such they could play a role
in spreading knowledge of improved techniques which neither
the illiterate warrior class nor the illiterate peasant class could:

> If one is looking at the earliest mills, watermills or windmills or
> for progress in farming techniques, one often sees the religious
> orders in the vanguard.[77]

This section of the feudal ruling class could also do something
that no one else could—gain access to the writings on technology of the Greek and Roman worlds and of the Byzantine and
Arabic empires which existed alongside feudal Europe:

> It is characteristic of medieval Christiandom that it put to indus-
> trial use technical devices which in classical society had been
> known but left almost unused or regarded simply as toys.[78]

The important point was that on the ecclesiastical demesnes

a literate group of exploiters were responsible for supervising the labour of the mass of direct producers. This seems to have given a boost to developments in technology through to the 13th or 14th century. Recent investigations of medieval science and technology have emphasised the extent to which thinkers previously thought of as 'scholastic' were, in fact, deeply concerned with providing solutions to practical problems.[79] The feudal lords, lay and ecclesiastical, were a very wasteful ruling class, absorbing much of the hard won produce of a poor society through their own parasitic consumption, and despoiling much more with their endless wars.[80] They did, however, preside over a certain development of production:

> The investment in agriculture which did occur must be viewed as resulting largely from the activities of the landlords and others who cultivated and produced on a large scale. Four to five percent of revenues went into gross investment and a level of one or two percent for new investment is probably quite representative.[81]

This is a very low level of investment compared to that found under modern capitalism. But, nevertheless, it was still investment, and it is wrong to give the impression, as many commentators have, that no investment at all took place, that 'feudal lords did not have the option of increasing their incomes through capital investments that would raise the productivity of labour…'[82]

The growth of the feudal forces of production

Our knowledge about the organisation of production in early medieval times is very scant. But that does not justify claims that there was no advance:[83]

> The prime event in Europe's history during the early middle ages was the development, between the 6th and the late 8th centuries, of a novel system of agriculture appropriate to the northern lands. As the elements of it emerged, consolidated into a new pattern of cultivation and spread, it proved to be the most productive agrarian method, in relation to manpower, that the world has seen.[84]

The first major innovation was the use of a heavy wheeled plough which could deal with heavy soils instead of the light scratch plough of the ancient world. The new plough spread from the Slavs in the 6th century to the Po valley in the 7th century, Germany in the 8th century and Britain in the 9th century. Its spread revolutionised both agricultural techniques and the relations among cultivators in manorial communities: the new plough was most efficiently used if peasants tilled strips of land rather than squarish fields, and, needing eight, rather than two, oxen to pull it, encouraged peasants to pool their resources through a new emphasis on communal cooperation. The spread of the heavy plough was followed by further major innovations—the adoption of a three field system, in which only a third of the land was left fallow at any point in time, a new emphasis on the use of animal dung to reinvigorate the soil, the planting of pulses which raised the protein content of people's diet and the cultivation of oats which enabled some peasants at least to replace the slow ox with the much faster, although more expensive, horse:

> The heavy plough, the open fields, the new integration of agriculture and herding, three field rotation, the modern horse harness, nailed horse shoes and the whipple tree [for pulling horse drawn vehicles—CH] had combined into a total system of agrarian exploitation by the year 1100 to provide a zone of peasant prosperity stretching right across Northern Europe from the Atlantic to the Dnieper.[85]

These changes produced a considerable increase in productivity per head and in the yield of seed corn. Georges Duby estimates grain yields as being only 2:1 in the 9th century—so that half the grain harvested had to be saved for planting the following year, however many people were starving. But yields had reached 3:1 or 4:1 in in the 12th century.[86] 'There is reason to believe that a general rise in productivity occurred between the 9th and 12th centuries…of 100 percent'.[87]

George Duby, in his study of medieval agriculture, goes so far as to claim:

> A great change in productivity, the only one in history until the great advances of the 18th and 19th centuries, occurred in Western Europe between the Carolingian period and the dawn of the 13th century.[88]

The feudal mode of production was characterised by a slow development of the forces of production, but not by stagnation.

Apologists for feudalism—as for all class societies—claim

that the exploiting class deserved the thanks of the exploited class by developing production in this way. Socialists reject this claim. The innovations and investments of the feudal period were based upon the labour which the feudal lords had stolen from the peasants. But Marx and Engels were quite right to point out that each form of class society does play a certain 'progressive' role for a period. While the productivity of labour is low, the mass of the population must live so close to subsistence level as to be unable to sustain through their own volition the investments needed to increase productivity and to provide for the development of culture and civilisation. This will only occur when one small section of society gains control over that surplus over and above what is needed to keep the mass at the subsistence level. Then, although it may well waste much of the surplus, it will enable some at least to be invested.

Under feudalism the waste, particularly on the continual warfare between the feudal lords, was enormous. Nevertheless, the mode of production was dynamic enough for western European society, over a 1,000 year period, to recover from the economic collapse of late Roman times and to outstrip, in terms of technology and productivity, societies like those of China and the Islamic empires that had initially been far in advance of it.

Trade, the towns and medieval industry

Early feudalism was, as we have seen, an almost entirely rural society. But the rise of towns was not something extraneous to this society—it was a result of its internal development. The growth in the productivity of both land and labour in the 10th and 11th centuries provided the lords with a growing surplus of agricultural products. They could use this surplus either for personal consumption or for waging war against other lords. In either case, it was to their advantage to exchange some of it for products from outside their own demesne—for more specialised foodstuffs and non-agricultural products such as weapons, fine clothing or building materials. And so they encouraged the growth of new centres of trade and handicraft production—new towns. While most of the old Roman cities disappeared or declined into simple religious and administrative centres, a whole range of new cities emerged. As Le Goff writes:

81

Venice, Florence, Genoa, Pisa, even Milan, Paris, Bruges, Ghent and London, let alone Hamburg or Lübeck, were essentially creations of the middle ages...

The towns were born not only out of the reawakening of trade, but also out of the growth of agriculture in the west, which was beginning to supply urban centres with a better supply of food and manpower.

Of course, the towns attracted new men who had escaped from the land... Yet they were joined by members of the ruling class, who helped notably by lending money which they alone had at the outset...[89]

The towns, then, were initially an outgrowth of the rural society around them. They were a product of feudalism. Yet at the same time they contained new ways by which a minority in society could gain control of the surplus. Merchants could cream off some of the surplus previously in the hands of the feudal lords through trade, and in the process transform themselves into a new class, with different interests to the old rural ruling class. And the towns also contained new ways of creating wealth, through handicraft production, again quite different to the agricultural production of the countryside.

Even when non-agricultural production was concentrated in the feudal demesnes, there had been some technical advance. The new, growing medieval towns witnessed much more advance:

From about the 6th century, Europe began to show innovations in technology more significant than those found in the more elaborate neighbouring and kindred cultures of Byzantium and Islam. By the middle of the 14th century, after the invention of the mechanical clock had increased the number of artisans skilled in making intricate metal machines, Europe surpassed China and seized global leadership in technology. Some inventions were borrowed, notably from China, others were internally generated. The end result of medieval developments was the physical equipment of the early modern capitalist world.[90]

Among the most notable innovations of the feudal centuries were the crank (enabling much wider use of the water mill), the spinning wheel, the lathe, the development of dyes, printing and paper making, the invention of eyeglasses (so enormously extending the active life of the literate minority), new shipbuilding

82

technologies, and the compass.

All of these led to big leaps in productivity. In villages, for every five people the water mill freed about one person day's labour a week.[91] In towns the use of the mill for fulling, ie beating cloth to finish it, saved even greater amounts of labour. And as time went on the mill was applied to an increasing number of purposes—to iron working, for example. The use of the compass doubled the number of journeys a ship from Venice or Genoa could make to the Levant in a year.

The increases in productivity associated with the spinning wheel, more advanced looms or new techniques of metal working may seem small compared with the 10,000 percent increases seen in the industrial revolution. But they could bring about a doubling or trebling of productivity, an enormous gain for people whose labour barely enabled them to rise above the subsistence level. This gain is significant enough not to be simply ignored as all sides in the Sweezy-Wallerstein-Brenner debate tend to do.

Town, country and feudalism

As centres of trade and manufacturing, the towns began to develop according to a dynamic different to the rural feudal society which had given birth to them. Whereas 10th century feudalism was bound to the logic of autarchic manors which produced the subsistence of both the exploited and the exploiting class, the towns were bound from the beginning to the logic of the commodity, of goods which had to be exchanged if their owners were to feed themselves. The means of exchange, money, which had been of marginal significance in the feudal society of the early 10th century was of central significance to the towns which had grown up within it by the 12th century. Le Goff summarises the whole process very well:

> In order to come into existence the towns needed a favourable rural environment, but gradually as they develop they exercise an ever larger attraction over the surrounding area extending in proportion to their demands. The urban population was a group of consumers who only took part in farming as a sideline and who needed to be fed... Around the towns more land was cleared and yields rose, the more so since towns not only drew food from their surrounding areas but also took away people. Emigration from the

83

countryside to the town between the 10th and the 14th century was one of the most important events which took place in Christian Europe. What is certain in any case is the towns forged a new society out of the varied human elements which they took in.[92]

The towns were part of feudal society, and the urban classes shared many of the attitudes prevalent in society at large. Urban ruling groups often turned themselves into feudal proprietors in surrounding rural areas. The feudal lords often lived in and influenced the towns. The urban upper classes imitated the lifestyles of the feudal nobles. 'Yet little by little urban society succeeded in substituting its own impulse for the catchwords of the countryside'.[93]

This was shown by an important shift in the ideological centres of the feudal world. While until the 12th century the dominant ideas were pumped out from monasteries which were themselves based on rural manors, 'in the 13th century the spiritual leaders, the Dominicans and Franciscans, established themselves in the towns and governed souls from their pulpits and their university chairs'.[94]

From now on the towns took over the role of directing, inspiring, and developing ideas. At first this manifested itself in the economy. Even if the town initially had been a trading centre, a commercial nexus, a market, its basic function in economic terms was production. Towns were workshops; more importantly, it was in these workshops that the division of labour originated. In the countryside in the early middle ages all forms of production were concentrated within the manor, even if some skilled craftsmanship did find a home there too... However, in the towns such specialisation was carried to its limits. The craftsman had ceased to be primarily, or even additionally, a peasant, and the burgess had ceased to be primarily or additionally a landowner.[95]

The medieval towns could not have developed without the prior advance in techniques and productivity in the countryside. But in the towns the possibilities for further growth of productivity were much higher than in the countryside. Whereas the productivity of agricultural labour took two or three centuries to double, the productivity of urban craftsmen could be increased much more quickly by adopting new techniques—or often old techniques developed, but not used, in Roman times. The basis existed for the owners of urban workshops to expand their wealth at a faster rate than the initially much wealthier rural lords. What was required for them to do so was to find a workforce which itself had no control of the means of production and therefore would work for little more than a subsistence wage. Such a workforce was to be found among recent arrivals from the countryside, from ex-serfs and their families. From the beginning there was, therefore, the potential for turning means of production in the towns into capital and, with it, the potential for the self expansion of capital.

This potential was mostly not realised. There were objective obstacles. Handicraft production was still at the stage where it depended upon the much bigger agricultural sector of the economy to feed its workforce and buy much of its output. A succession of bad harvests could destroy its markets, at least temporarily, and with them the ability of the urban workforce to get the money to pay for food. A military campaign in the locality could have very much the same effect. In either case, an urban economy which had previously been flourishing could suddenly be devastated. Many a new shoot of urban handicraft production wilted in such a harsh environment.

There were other obstacles as well. The ideology of feudal society was not favourable to technical advance, even if it could not block it entirely. And the new urban classes, growing up within feudalism, more often than not adapted to its conservative attitudes. The owners of workshops would often seek to use political influence in the towns to provide a guaranteed income for themselves by imposing guild regulations which restricted competition. The journeymen who laboured in the workshops would fight against the introduction of new techniques which might threaten their jobs. Nevertheless, there were occasions in which new techniques of production were combined with new methods of employing 'free' wage labour on a big enough scale to create the beginnings of industry of a distinctly capitalist sort. This was true by the late 13th century in the two most economically advanced areas of Europe—in Flanders and in northern Italy:

In the early 14th century the belt of land which corresponds with the western part of modern Belgium and the north west corner of France contained a number of towns whose inhabitants lived on a highly developed woollen cloth industry. Bruges, Ghent, Ypres…Brussels

and Mallines, and Douai and Arras…were some of the most important. There are thought to have been at least 4,000 weavers alone,
apart from other allied trades, in the city of Ghent in the mid-14th
century. Industry on this scale led to the existence of substantial capitalists… The cloth towns, nearly all pure industrial centres…
developed on a large scale the characteristic physiognomy of the
modern city: commercial wealth contrasting with the relative poverty
of the numerous artisans and paid workers for whom the city bell
rang out the beginning of the working day.[96]

A contemporary chronicler claimed that in Florence, in
Northern Italy, the city's wool guild had over 200 workshops sup-
porting 30,000 people in the 1330s.[97] It is quite correct to stress
that these were embryos of a new mode of production, and that
like many other embryos they were often aborted. But every
embryo, whether aborted or not, influences the metabolism of the
body in which it finds itself. An important part of the reason
that feudalism in the 15th and 16th centuries was very different
to feudalism in Charlemagne's time was because of the way in
which the embryonic capitalist features of the towns had reacted
back upon the overwhelmingly rural societies from which they
had sprung.

Merchants and capitalism

Industrial capitalism made fleeting appearances during the
medieval period—appearances which were significant because
they occurred in the most economically advanced regions and
because they gave a foretaste of the future. But much more
important in general was merchants' capital. This has made the
question of the relationship of merchant capitalism to both feudal
and capitalist production a central one in all the debates over the
transition.[98]

The growth of towns arose from the growth of trade, which
was only possible with the marketisation of some production in
the countryside. But the growth of the towns in turn encouraged
further marketisation, creating as it did a section of the population which could not physically survive without trading its output
for food. The rise of the towns is thus synonymous with the rise
of commodity production.

Commodity production is not itself capitalism. It can grow up on the surface of non-capitalist societies, leaving old methods of production and exploitation intact. This, for instance, was true of trade in the Roman and Chinese empires. And even during the period of the ascendancy of capitalism as a world system, non-capitalist forms of exploitation could survive—in the latifundia of Latin America, in the slave plantations of the southern states of the United States, and in the vast labour camps of Stalin's gulag. So commodity production alone did not bring the feudal mode of production to an end. But that does not mean commodity production—and the class which organises the exchange of commodities, the merchant class—has no impact at all on the underlying forms of production and exploitation. The latifundia, the slave plantations and the labour camps were in fact products of the impact of a global system of commodity production.[99] So too was the transformation of the way in which feudal society was organised between the 10th century and the 14th century.

The rise of the market and the merchants in feudal society did not bring about an automatic transition to capitalism. But it did bring about transformations within feudalism which meant that, when the mode of production entered into deep crisis, capitalist development was one possible option. The merchants of the middle ages were concerned with the self expansion of their wealth (with M-M'). The easiest way for them to achieve this was by taking advantage of the imperfect development of the trading system, of the fact that there were substantial price differences from region to region. They could do this within the confines of a system of production run by other classes. But these differences in prices could not be relied on to provide substantial profits indefinitely. If other merchants entered the ring, then prices in the final market would fall and the self expansion of wealth would come to an end.

It was this which led the merchants to fight for political power in the towns and then to use this political power to rig the feudal market in their own favour—via monopolies, encouragement of wars against rivals, piracy, and so on. It was this too which led successful merchants to try to protect their accumulations of wealth by moving them from the cities and trade into land. They would usually end up trying to guarantee their future well being by buying themselves into the feudal ruling class. They developed all sorts of interests in compromising with the ruling powers of feudal society. To this extent there was a powerful conservative trend built into merchant capital. In the great revolutions of the 17th and 18th centuries most of the great merchants stood for 'moderate reform' and a few sided with the out and out defenders of the old order.

Yet at the same time the growing marketisation of the economy provided merchant capital with a way of expanding itself on a surer long term basis than through trade alone, a basis that was in contradiction to the feudal mode of production. For the impact of marketisation was to deprive growing numbers of people both in town and country of direct access to the means of production and to turn them into a potential pool of wage labour. Peasants who could not pay their rents sold their land and sought paid employment, journeymen who could not afford to set up as independent tradesmen were forced onto the urban labour market. Capitalist exploitation, based on 'free labour', became possible, but often this did not appear in its full form.

As Marx noted long ago,[100] the first fleeting appearances of a way of achieving the self expansion of capital which did not depend on accidents or monopolies were shortlived. The Flemish cloth industry declined after the late 14th century, the North Italian industries a century later. But that was not the end of merchant capital's attempts in this direction. The decline of urban industry in the face of general economic crisis and the resistance of the urban lower classes to increased exploitation were followed by the rise of rural handicraft production, very much under the direction of urban based merchants.

This was not usually fully capitalist production. The handicraft producers mostly owned their own means of production—the cottage in which they worked and the spinning wheel or loom they worked on. This enabled them to work at their own speed and to restrict their output to what was needed to provide themselves with their own basic needs—that is, to avoid being pulled into the endless treadmill of production for the sake of production, of the pursuit of the self expansion of their capital. But the merchant would control both the supply of raw materials to them and the marketing of their output. In this way he would be able to force them to surrender to him a portion of the value of their product.

As Jurgen Schlumbohm has pointed out,[101] it was a short step from this system (known in German as the *Kaufsystem*, ie buying system) to the putting out system (in German *Verlagsystem*) in which the merchant capitalist loans the direct producer raw materials in return for a guaranteed level of output. Once this has taken place, the direct producer is only in part his own master. He depends on others for some of his productive resources—and this enables them to dictate to him his tempo of work, to force him to accept, in part at least, subordination to the self expansion of capital. From here it is another short step to capitalist production proper, with the capitalist providing both the means and the materials of production.

In practice these three stages were always combined in various ways. In cloth manufacture, for instance, spinning and weaving might take place under the buying system, but certain finishing processes were carried out in workshops directly owned and supervised by the merchant capitalist. So for centuries there were hybrid, bastardised forms of production, in which elements of capitalist exploitation were mixed with elements of non-capitalist commodity production by individual craftsmen. But the tendency was for the element of direct capitalist control to grow over time:

> The putting out system did not entail an increased labour productivity. Yet the management of the different stages of production by a single entrepreneur opened up important opportunities for innovations.[102]

Since some of these innovations could only be achieved with the use of more expensive equipment that only the capitalist could buy, the buying system tended over centuries to give way to the putting out system, and the putting out system to capitalist production proper.

The development of industry in the countryside was no more an automatic or a smooth process than the earlier development in the medieval towns had been. Industry could only grow in rural areas to the extent that marketisation was already destroying the bonds which tied the whole rural population to agricultural production and forcing some of them to seek new sources of livelihood. Those urban classes who lost out by rural industrialisation tried to prevent it—for instance, using their political influence to press for state wide controls over production methods. The narrow base of the market for industrial output and the precariousness of the ability of the rural economy to provide food at prices which the new handicraft workers were able to afford could force expanding areas of rural industry into sudden crisis and even obliteration. The merchant capitalists could lose interest in productive activity and move their capital into speculative venture or land.

Yet by the late middle ages 'centres of dense rural industry developed in England, the southern low countries and southern Germany'.[103] Whereas in the 14th century only 4 percent of English wool was manufactured into cloth before export, with the rest serving as raw material for the Flemish and Italian urban based industries, by the mid-15th century 50 percent was manufactured and by the mid-16th century 86 percent:[104]

> Proto-industrialisation, on the one hand, was kept in check by rural relations of production and, on the other, it acted as a powerful ferment in the gradual disintegration of those relations. While feudal ties maintained their strength to varying degrees, relations of dependence that were essentially of a capitalist nature arose besides them in industrial regions. Often it was only a matter of time before merchant capital would shake off the remaining fetters of feudalism and enforce the formal freedom of labour.[105]

Where rural industries took off, they had an immediate impact on agricultural production. The demand of the handicraft producers for foodstuffs encouraged marketisation of agriculture, while the need of the urban based merchants to retain the services of the proto-industrial workforce led them to help it protect the rural producers against pressures for feudal services by the lords. The rulers of the towns, and the armed forces at their disposal, had a direct interest in undermining ties of feudal dependency in parts of the countryside:

> That industrial commodity production in the countryside was integrated less directly and less comprehensively into the feudal system than was agrarian production is most clearly illustrated by the fact that rent in kind and labour services could remain viable in agricultural production for the market, but rarely did either of them form the base of industrial commodity production.
>
> While in the eastern half of Europe, the production of grain for the market was dominated by the feudal system until the 19th century, it was much less widespread in industrial commodity production.[106]

What is more, the spread of rural industry served to create

direct social relations between the urban merchants and a rural middle class:

> Wealthy, business minded peasants...and members of the village 'bourgeoisie' often assumed a strategic function in the proto-industrialisation process...[as] the middle men between domestic producers and merchants. They constituted the personnel of the putting out system's infrastructure...[107]

The products of rural industry were not merely used in local trade, but in inter-regional and international trade. By the late 16th century trade in north and west Europe 'comprised mass consumption goods, above all cereals, livestock and copper from eastern Europe, and textiles and metal goods from western parts of the continent.[108] Merchant capital might have grown up within feudalism and might continually try to liquidate itself back into the feudal mode of production, but such developments also gave at least a section of it a powerful interest in identifying with a new mode of production, organised on quite a different basis to feudalism. And not only in relation to industry.

Brenner is right to say, following Marx, that there was growth of capitalist relations of production in parts of the countryside in this period. Sometimes this took the form of full blooded capitalist exploitation, the form which came to predominate in England. Sometimes, as in parts of France, a bastardised form prevailed: metayage, in which the landowner (often a bourgeois from the town) advanced half the stock and received half the crop which he would then market. In either case, what happened in the countryside was not something distinct from the development of the towns and of merchant capital. The growing specialisation of production in the countryside could only occur if there were growing trading networks, influencing the direction of agriculture as well as industry. A key role in these networks was played by a growing number of small towns, where new groups of traders could operate without any impediment from the guilds of the bigger towns. Rodney Hilton has shown how important these could be in medieval England, clashing with feudal lords even though these had often helped establish them.[109] Georges Duby tells how changes in the system of husbandry:

> were symptomatic of the opening of the country economy to exchanges, and went hand in hand with the gradual penetration of

money and credit. They stimulated the growth of a host of small
market towns inhabited by dealers in wine, grain and cattle, and
moneylenders. And these changes went deepest in regions close
to towns and to lines of communication.[110]

Agriculture was beginning to be transformed even before the
demographic crisis of the 14th century—and long before the
twofold outcome of the class struggle which Brenner claims
alone could permit any development of the productive forces.
After the first quarter of the 13th century, 'among those in charge
of agricultural production appeared many men well versed in the
rational methods of management and who were as attentive to the
operations of the market as they were to the theories of agriculture'.[111] The tendency to production for exchange 'rapidly
intensified in the 13th century... The play of commercial operations in the countryside on the eve of the 14th century was
astonishingly widespread and vigorous'.[112] This turn to commodity production was accompanied by changes in production
methods:

> Towards the end of the 13th century some remarkable changes in
> regions where economic expansion was taking place come to
> light. They all bear testimony to the desire to work the cultivated
> lands in a more rational manner and for greater profit.[113]

By the 15th century 'every town had its butchers, who were at
the same time entrepreneurs, cattle merchants, meat merchants
and leather merchants, all of them prosperous, the new men of
the pastoral economy and its absolute masters'.[114] No wonder Le
Goff describes the 'small towns' as the 'new active element'
giving direction to society as a whole as Europe recovered from
the Black Death in the 15th century.[115]

It is wrong to see merchant capital, as Pirenne, Sweezy and the
others tend to do, as the unambiguous agent of a new mode of
production within feudalism. Merchant capital was bound by a
thousand ties to the system out of which it grew and therefore
continually tended to sink back into that system. But it is also
wrong to see it, as Brenner does, as simply a force cementing
feudal ties. In fact, it both perpetuated the society it grew out of
and tended to undermine that society. It was, as Kriedte puts it,
'Janus faced', looking to the future as well as the past. This
enabled it (or at least sections of it) to play a very important role

in dissolving feudal ties. But it also meant that it was an obstacle to the full development of industrial capitalism which had, in the 18th century, to wage a struggle with it for hegemony before full blooded capitalist development could take off.[116]

The crisis of feudalism

Pre-capitalist class societies have known crises just as deep as any known by capitalism. This is clearly the case if you just look at the demographic devastation which occurred with the collapse of the Roman Empire in the west, at the height of the medieval period in the 14th century, or across continental Europe in the 17th century. But the cause of the crises was quite different to that under capitalism.

Capitalist crises have occurred every ten years or so as accumulation and production, both in industry and agriculture, outstrip the source of profits to the capitalist class. Feudal crises, by contrast, occurred every few centuries rather than every few years, and arose because society's demand for resources went beyond the capacity of the existing forces of production, especially in the countryside. Put crudely, the number of mouths to be fed grew more rapidly than the food supply and mass hunger resulted. This crisis has sometimes been called a 'Malthusian' or 'Neo-Malthusian' crisis, after the English clergyman who insisted at the beginning of the 19th century that humanity could never improve its lot because starvation would always result. The title is a poor one, because it was a particular, class directed way of organising production which led to the shortages of food, not any innate feature of human society.

Feudalism, as we have seen, advanced the forces of production, but in a very wasteful and therefore a very slow way. The advance of the forces of production was accompanied by a growth in population: conditions of relative prosperity led people in the countryside to marry earlier and have larger families; the growth of an exchangeable surplus encouraged the growth of the towns and with them a new urban population. Since there were large areas of untilled countryside (forests and swamps) under early feudalism, the growing number of people were easily fed at first as the expanding peasantry cleared and cultivated new land and as the slow spread of improved techniques increased yields on old land. But a point was eventually reached (towards the end of the 13th century and again towards the end of the 16th century) at which the supply of uncleared land began to run out. At this point the only way for the increased rural population to make a living was either to work marginal, relatively unproductive bits of land or to try to increase the output of other land without worrying about exhausting its fertility. In this way it was possible to keep output rising for a period, but not for very long. As yields on overfarmed land began to fall, it only required a poorer than average harvest to plunge the whole of society into famine. The crisis was not simply a 'demographic' one. It was intensified by the very feudal relations of production which had enabled production to rise in previous centuries. From being a spur to the development of the productive forces in the early feudal period these were now increasingly a drag on them.

A huge portion of the output of their serfs went into providing a rising level of conspicuous consumption for the feudal lords. Technical advances meant that armies could be larger and wars more far ranging than before—a further drain on society's resources. The rise of the towns provided a source of borrowing which allowed feudal lords to consume and fight beyond their means, at least up to a point: 'the poorer and middling members of the knightly class...got into debt faster than they could get out of it'.[117]

In the towns themselves a growing urban upper class itself consumed conspicuously, with its own retinues of servants, its own private armies, its own dependence on a proliferation of luxury trades, all of which had to be paid for and fed. The growth within the framework of feudalism of the new, exchange oriented forms of economic activity exacerbated the crisis, although in a contradictory way. It led, as we have seen, to increased concern with the productivity of labour and land. It provided opportunities for wage labour for the poorest section of the peasantry and so put off the moment at which they were driven to starvation. But it also diverted land from producing the staple foodstuff, grain, into providing marketable luxuries for the towns and the upper classes—wool, wine and meat:

> The entrepreneurs succeeded in building up units directly linked with trade; they went on improving their tools and perfecting techniques. In order to intensify grain production, they applied more complex rotational systems and engaged more labourers

to till the soil more thoroughly. Nevertheless their specific interests were the vineyards, the woodland, the grassland, and the management of their flocks which yielded the larger part of their profits.[118]

This intensified the factors leading to crisis while concealing them from view:

Between 1275 and 1330...arable land ceased to grow at the expense of the waste. This did not prevent the rural economy as a whole from wearing at this moment an air of solid prosperity. But nevertheless we notice that the antagonism between the small country people and the increasing band of entrepreneurs becomes sharper...[119]

While all this was happening, the ideology of the ruling class was less and less capable of coming to terms with the changes which were taking place. It increasingly came to reflect the pampered position which the feudal lords had attained, divorced from the world of production, concerned only with rank, honour and the defence of hereditary position. The creative period of medieval thought gave way to the sterile phase of scholasticism proper. The superstructures which had once overseen the growth of social production became more expensive to maintain—and ensured that, once social production began to falter, the crisis that resulted was on an immense scale.

Economic crisis could rapidly have political effects which made the economic crisis worse. In the countryside the different members of the feudal ruling class sought to protect their incomes by increased pressure on the peasants (which pushed the poorest peasants into ever greater poverty) and by increased military activity as each attempted to seize land from the other. In the cities there were increasingly bitter conflicts between the mass of the population, hard hit by rising food prices, and the handful of very rich families who held power. Wars and civil wars brought military devastation to an already impoverished society. And in the wake of hunger and war came diseases, above all the bubonic plague, which cut a huge swathe through the population. The crisis pushed society backward. The population halved in the space of a few years. Whole villages were deserted as their inhabitants died or fled. Vast tracts of countryside passed out of cultivation. Urban industry declined as the demand for its products fell.

To this extent the crisis of the 14th century had some features in common with the crisis of the late Roman Empire and the less demographically disastrous crisis of the Carolingian 9th century. But there was a difference. The development of the forces of production meant that towns did survive, even if in a weakened form. The trade networks remained intact. And so did industry, although it often moved to the countryside in search of cheaper labour. Indeed, once recovery from the immediate demographic catastrophe of the mid-14th century took place, industry was helped by its effects: the supply of foodstuffs, especially grain, was now greater than the demand from a diminished population, food prices fell relative to those of manufactured goods, and the poorer peasants could make a better living through rural handicrafts than through tilling the land.

All this meant that an alternative could emerge from the crisis of the 14th century to the feudal cycle of expansion and collapse. The alternative lay in carrying to its logical extreme the marketisation of output that had emerged in the previous centuries, so that not only goods but also labour power became a commodity. So it was that the period of recovery from the crisis of the 14th century saw in parts of western Europe the growth of rural industries controlled by merchant capitalists, on a greater scale than ever before. This period also saw in certain towns the growth of new industries, organised on capitalist lines in a much more sophisticated way than previously—most notably printing, paper making, shipbuilding and coal mining. It also saw the spread of the organised market system (controlled by merchants, big or small) which encouraged better off peasants to employ wage labour to produce much more than they needed for their own immediate consumption, so encouraging some feudal lords to protect their revenues through leasing lands to such peasants rather than through feudal dues.

Capitalism began to emerge not as merchant capitalism (the Pirenne-Sweezy version) or as agrarian capitalism (the Brenner version) but as a network of productive units in both handicrafts (in town and country) and agricultural production using free labour separated to varying degrees from real control over the means and materials of production, a network bound together by the activity of a section of merchant capital which itself was centred on the towns.

The transitional society and the absolutist state

There has been much debate about the character of western European society—and English society in particular—from the 15th century onwards, with Dobb and Anderson,[120] for instance, insisting it remained feudal, and Sweezy arguing it was based on a 'petty commodity producing mode of production'.[121] But the important point was that it was a society in transition, with both feudal and capitalist forms of exploitation existing side by side, and in many cases intermingling.

The two forms were both complementary (as when a feudal lord used some of his wealth to take part in commercial ventures using some waged labour, or when a merchant used the profits from the putting out system to set himself up with a manor) and contradictory (as when merchants and feudal lords fought physically for political dominance of great cities). What is more, they operated according to different dynamics. The relatively slow growth of the forces of production under feudal forms of exploitation, compared with the faster growth under capitalist forms, meant that the balance between the two was continually changing. Whereas the balance of the economy in France, say, was overwhelmingly towards feudalism in the 15th century, by the late 18th century it was much more tilted in a capitalist direction.

This changing balance had strong effects on the politics of the period. One element of feudal society, the monarchy, tried to strengthen itself by balancing between the feudal lords and the different urban classes. The feudal monarchy had been a weak central force, exercising power only in so far as it could persuade the nobles who held real power in each locality to accept its rule. In the late 15th and early 16th centuries both old monarchs (as in France, and England) and new rulers (like the Medicis in the Italian city state of Florence) began to construct absolutisms, in which their power overrode that of the local nobles and urban oligarchies alike. They were able to do so because they used the towns to counterbalance the power of the rural lords—and, if necessary, the middle classes in the towns as a counterbalance to the oligarchies. Symbolic of the change was the construction by the French monarchy alongside the old feudal lords (the *nobles d'épee*) of a new aristocracy to man its state bureaucracy (the

97

noblesse de robe) drawn from bourgeois families.

None of these changes could have occurred had recovery from the crisis of the 14th century not been associated with a rise in the importance of the urban ruling and middle classes compared to the feudal lords, a rise dependent upon a further spread of commodity production and within that of elements of capitalist production:

> The industrial and commercial world does not present the same picture of general decay as the seigniorial world... Cities such as Florence, Venice, Bruges, London or Nuremberg acquired a prominence apparently greater than they had enjoyed earlier, even though they were smaller communities...[122]

Perry Anderson quite rightly stresses:

> It is significant that the years 1450 to 1500, which saw the emergence of the first prodromes [forerunner—CH] of unified absolute monarchies in the west, were also those in which the long crisis of the feudal economy was surmounted by recombination of production factors in which, for the first time, specifically urban technological advances played a leading role.[123]

But the logical inference to be drawn from this observation is that absolutism was not simply a changed 'form of feudal exploitation' and its function was not simply 'the repression of the peasant and plebian masses'.[124] It was rather a political form which, in Engels' words, could arise in a period when 'the warring classes balance each other so nearly that the state power, as ostensible mediator, acquires for the moment a certain degree of independence of both'.[125]

The state administrators had an interest in the continuation of feudalism: after all part of their own income came from direct feudal exploitation of peasants on the monarchy's own lands. But they also had an interest in the further development of trade and of direct capitalist forms of exploitation: these provided them with a expanding urban tax base. Finally, they had an interest in maintaining the balance between the two: then they could use the power of the feudal lords to deal with any town which stepped out of line, and they could use the power of the towns to force the feudal lords to let them have (through taxation) part of the surplus product of the peasantry which otherwise would have been absorbed completely by feudal dues. So it is in this period that the state does not simply adjust to advances in capitalist forms of production which had already taken place, but encourages such advances itself, sometimes from scratch.

It was as Janus faced as merchant capital. Like the great merchants, those who rose to eminence and wealth out of administering the state were continually caught between two facts: the quickest way to make wealth was to identify with the anti-feudal forces, but the best way to preserve it was to sink it back into land.

So, even when the administrators themselves were bourgeois in origin, as with the *noblesse de robe* in France, they tended over time to revert back to feudal forms of exploitation. Similarly, in England key figures in running the Tudor state came from non-lordly backgrounds, yet 100 years later their descendants were well established as landowners.

Even this was not the end of the matter. For if merchants and state administrators were continually falling back into the methods of the feudal ruling class, this class itself was also beginning, in part, to adapt to methods of capitalist exploitation. Few feudal lords themselves became either capitalist farmers or capitalist industrialists. But many began to see their future as better assured if they were landlords to capitalist farmers than to feudal peasants, and many began to see the advantages of doing deals with merchant capitalists.

The contradictory role of the state in this period is shown most sharply by looking at how it used its 'bodies of armed men'. For the feudalists their function was to fight for land, the source of feudal wealth. Where this land was did not really matter to the feudal lord. So the typical feudal war was part of a dynastic struggle to secure scattered territories for one or other monarchy—as with the battles between German princes, French kings and the popes for control of Sicily in the 13th century, or the Hundred Years War between French, English and Burgundian rulers in the 14th and early 15th century.

By contrast, merchant capitalists were concerned with securing a hold on their trading networks. As urban and rural industry developed, and with it capitalist agriculture, this meant trying to bind together adjacent geographic regions within a single, stable political framework: in short, seeking to establish some sort of national state. Wars, for them, should be national wars, aimed at consolidating the territory of the nation and opening new markets for trade. The degree to which the rulers of the absolutist state looked backwards to feudalism or forwards to capitalist methods of exploitation was shown by the degree to which they fought one kind of war or the other. There were absolutisms (Spain, for example) where dynastic wars predominated. But there were more advanced cases (England in the 16th century, France in the 18th) in which commercial and 'national' considerations came to predominate.

The class struggle and the transition

The growth of capitalist forms of exploitation at the expense of feudal forms was not some automatic process. The old feudal ruling classes' power was weakened by the crisis of the 14th century. While land had been in increasingly short supply under pressure from a growing population, it had been able to keep a land hungry peasantry subjugated without too much resort to physical coercion. Now suddenly, with the rural population halved, discontented peasants could flee one lord and easily find land elsewhere unless faced with vicious repression.

But this did not mean the feudal ruling classes just sat back and watched their power decline. As Brenner quite rightly emphasises, they attempted to use force to make up for their economic losses. The result was a series of large scale and violent clashes between the exploited and the exploiters, starting with the Jacquerie, a huge and bloody peasant rising in the Paris region in 1358. Then there was the revolt of the *ciompi* (wool carders) in Florence in 1378, the risings of weavers in Ghent and Bruges of 1379-82, the peasants' revolt in England in 1381, and the rising of the *maillotins* (the lower classes, so called because they armed themselves with mallets) of Paris in 1382.[126]

None of these struggles was victorious in the sense of immediately breaking the power of either the lords in the countryside or the oligarchies in the towns. But they did show there were limits beyond which the old feudal ruling classes could not go in their attempt to make up for their losses as a result of the crisis. Within the next half century there was a decline in direct feudal authority over both peasants and townspeople right across western Europe.[127] The most extreme expression of direct lordly control, the demesnes tilled by serf labour, virtually disappeared in this period. By the beginning of the 16th century Europe had recovered from the crisis. Population was growing right across the continent, and lands which had been abandoned 150 years before were now once more beginning to be cultivated. Grain prices stopped falling and began to rise in what has been called the 'inflation of the 16th century'.

If the weakening of feudal ties had simply been an automatic response to the crisis of the 14th century, then there should have been a regrowth of feudal ties in the 16th century. This did occur in much of eastern Europe—where there was a return to demesne production using forced labour—and in parts of Italy and the Iberian peninsular. But it did not occur in much of western Europe.

How is the difference to be explained? Not simply in terms of the growth of marketisation, since much of the output of the east European landed estates was sold. Brenner argues that what matters is the different outcome to the class struggle in the two regions. But this begs the question as to why the anti-feudal forces were more successful in the west than the east and, in the west itself, more successful in England than in France.[128]

We cannot explain the difference without reference to the simple fact that urban development and rural industrial development were more pronounced in the west than in the east. This did not mean that either the urban oligarchy or the urban middle and lower classes always supported the peasants against the feudal lords.[129] But they did represent centres of power independent of the feudal lords which made it more difficult for the latter to impose their interests on the whole of society or, one expression of this, to always bend the state bureaucracy to their will. In eastern Europe, where the towns and the urban classes were relatively weak, the state did indeed function simply as the expression of a centralised feudalism, helping the nobility to crush the peasants, reimpose serfdom and extend its demesnes. In western Europe, faced with a different balance of forces in society as a whole, the state did not give such unambiguous backing to the forces of feudalism, thus aiding the peasantry to retain much of their freedom. Caught between the past and the future, the monarchical states facilitated the growth of capitalist forms of exploitation, but also became a drag upon them at key moments in history. Then bitter class struggles alone could determine whether society moved forwards or backwards. And these struggles involved bitter clashes between rival exploiting classes as well as between the exploiters and the exploited classes.

The transition and ideology

These transformations in society necessarily found expression in the realm of ideas. People began to try to come to terms with the changes which were taking place in their lives, with some trying to slow down these changes and others to speed them up. It is hardly surprising that the late 15th and 16th centuries saw the spread of ideas which challenged, at first implicitly and then explicitly, the ideological centre of feudalism, the Catholic church.

The Reformation was not, of course, a simple adoption of pro-capitalist ideas by people opposed to feudalism. The transition period involved the emergence of a range of classes and social groups—the urban oligarchies, the middle ranking urban merchants and handicraft proprietors, the urban poor, the new layer of rich, labour-employing peasants, those they employed, the administrators of different states—alongside the old classes of feudalism. Each of these groups could only achieve its goals by making and unmaking alliances with other groups, and each, in the process, fell to some degree under the influence of other groups. There was no clear notion of what was to replace medieval society amongst any of these groups. But there was a sense that things were changing, that the old religious conceptions and institutions no longer fitted.

So, Jan Hus, Luther, Calvin or John Knox could preach doctrines which meant different things to different social groupings. But such ideas also provided at least a temporary basis for uniting such groupings in opposition to the old order of things to such an extent that people were prepared to fight and die for what they believed. Those who were most radical in their religious reinterpretation of the world tended to be those who wanted it changed most—whether, as with the radical Hussites or the Anabaptists, to an egalitarian classless society, or, as with the more sober minded Calvinists, to a society based upon commodity production and the relentless attempt to accumulate capital.

These new ideas were the product of urban based preachers. But they had an impact on rural as well as urban classes. This is not surprising. The market networks which had grown up, under the control of big and small merchants, to unite producers and consumers in town and country were also networks through which ideas could travel. Verbal intercourse accompanied commercial intercourse—between the merchants of a city, the nobles, wealthier peasants, rural handicraft manufacturers and small town traders of its hinterland. Single languages replaced hotchpotches of local dialects within each regional trading network. The more trade developed, the more this took written forms. Part of the ideological challenge to the medieval world lay in people putting across their ideas in these new languages, asserting them as national languages as opposed to the Latin of the feudal church. The networks which carried trade were soon also carrying dissident ideological works of various kinds, from the tracts of Martin Luther or Thomas Munzer to the satirical books of Rabelais.

The town united the countryside (or at least part of the countryside) behind it in presenting an ideological as well as an economic alternative to the feudal world—something which is inexplicable if you see the transition, as Brenner does, as originating purely in the countryside.

The transition and the first great revolutions

The transitional society combined contradictory forces, between which monarchical states tried to balance. But however high the state raised itself for a certain period, it could not stop the forces moving so far in opposite directions as to bring it crashing down eventually. There were elements in the old feudal ruling class which looked back to old methods of exploitation whenever society entered into crisis. And this happened on a European scale in the 17th century, in much the same way as it had done three centuries before.

The elements looking to the old feudalism had already reorganised themselves with the ideology and institutions of the Counter-Reformation (for example, the Jesuits and the inquisition) in the second half of the 16th century. They had enormous financial backing from the Spanish monarchy, a feudal state which nevertheless controlled most of the gold flowing into Europe from Latin America. In the first half of the 17th century they sought to preserve society as they knew it from the contagion of the new ways and the new ideas by waging a war across half of Europe—the Thirty Years War.

The two epicentres of this struggle were Holland and Bohemia. Neither was by any means a pure capitalist state. Far from it. In both, elements of the old nobility retained considerable influence.   103

They were ruled by Estates—representatives of both the lords and the towns—not by revolutionary assemblies. But in both, a substantial section of the nobility identified with new ways of producing wealth, through trade and through urban and rural manufacturing, and through agriculture in which feudal dues played a very small part.[130] The Estates in neither country were keen for the great struggles in which they found themselves. The Bohemians tried to avoid war, and the Dutch waited 12 years before joining in. But the sheer scale of the feudal reaction gave them no choice. Polisensky has described the conflict as of 'two civilisations in ideological conflict'.[131] But he has gone on to insist:

> It would be a crass oversimplification to contend that the war was a collision between the champions of capitalism and the bourgeoisie on the one hand, and the representatives of the old regime on the other. These two models were only the poles in a whole complex struggle, the centres around which were forged two powerful political camps.[132]

By the time the war ended in 1648 the issues which had led to it were half forgotten. Absolutist Catholic France became the main obstacle, for its own great power reasons, to the all out victory of the reactionary forces. Bohemia had long since been conquered for feudalism, and the devastation of the war's main battleground, Germany, halved its population and set back its economic development by a century. Only in Holland did the forces standing for a new, thoroughly bourgeois, organisation of society survive intact.

Even before the Thirty Years War was over, a similarly decisive but confused struggle was taking place in England and Scotland. A section of the old ruling class was inspired by the general reactionary ideology emanating from Spain. The king, Charles I, tried to go against the foreign policy interests of those social forces associated with the new ways of making wealth and to rule in an arbitrary manner in opposition to their desires. He was soon confronted by an armed coalition, made up of sections of the aristocracy, much of the rural gentry, many (but not the topmost) merchants and the middling classes of both town and country.

As in Bohemia and Holland, this coalition did not want to push the struggle to the limit. But also as in those cases, the old order did not give them much choice. As the king ratted on

compromise after compromise, the leadership of the oppositional camp fell into the hands of those who no longer looked
for a slightly reformed version of the old transitional society,
but to one which had gone much further on the way towards
capitalism.

The crisis of the 17th century meant that all the different elements which made up the transitional society were thrown into
conflict with each other—aristocrats, gentry and rural manufacturers in the countryside, big merchants and small merchants and
manufacturers in the towns, the monarchy and the classes
between which it had previously balanced. In the confused battles which followed no class was initially clear on its own long
term interests. But the very severity of the political crisis forced
people to try to see through the fog to some resolution of the
crisis. And for those who did not want a reversion to feudalism,
there was only one such way—a policy which would steadfastly
develop the new forms of production and exploitation as opposed
to the old. The genius of Cromwell in the English Revolution lay
in his instinctive grasp of the direction in which society had to go
and in his ability to mobilise a coalition of forces which could
achieve this.

But the precondition for such a coalition was precisely the
networks of people committed to the new ways—the lesser merchants, yeoman farmers employing wage labour, the promoters of
urban and rural handicrafts and industries. Interestingly, the
strongest support for the revolution came from London, the sea-
ports and those rural areas which produced agricultural and/or
manufactured goods for the market. Cromwell could build out of
these a coalition which could beat the king and, in presenting a
programme to unite them in struggle, push the development of the
sort of society they represented further forward.

Wherever such leadership was not able to construct a coalition
of forces capable of victory in this way (whether for objective
or subjective reasons), the result was that society was pushed
backward. This had already happened in late 15th century Italy,
where the forward development of the city states came to an
end with the French invasion of 1494. It happened, as we have
seen, in Bohemia and Germany in the Thirty Years War. And it
happened in France in 1648, when a confused revolt, the Fronde,
drove the monarchy from Paris but did not coalesce into a force
with any programme for developing French society.

Capitalism and colonies

In the period of the first great revolutions capitalism proper, based on the routine exploitation of 'free labour' in industry and on the land, was still overshadowed by merchant capitalism. And merchant capitalism was increasingly identified with the carving out of colonial empires from which enormous riches flowed back into Europe, riches which made it much easier for the rising bourgeoisie to buy over or subvert the old ruling classes. It is this which has led Sweezy, Wallerstein and other authors such as Gunder Frank to see the secret of capitalist development as lying in the 'unequal exchange' established between western Europe and the rest of the world. But that leaves two vital questions unexplained. First, why were western European states able to exercise such a stranglehold over the rest of the world? Second, why did some states experience successful capitalist development based upon such 'unequal' trade, but not others? Spain and Portugal were, after all, in advance of Britain, Holland and France in establishing colonial empires, but suffered impoverishment, not growth, in the 17th and 18th centuries. And Holland was a greater trading centre than England in the mid-17th century, but thereafter fell behind in the advance to full blooded capitalist development.

It is only possible to answer these questions by recognising that the key to international influence lay in developments in the domestic economies, which were then further enhanced by colonial control and 'unequal exchange'. Western Europe's rulers and merchants could only impose their will elsewhere in the world because already, after the crisis of the 14th century, the means of production were more advanced in Europe than in the parts of the globe they subjugated. The growth of the new empires led to economic advance in Holland and England precisely because more productive capitalist and semi-capitalist forms of exploitation were beginning to emerge there rather than in Spain and Portugal. England overtook Holland because Dutch merchant capitalism was not able to establish networks of rural manufacturing under its control as its English rivals did.[133]

There is an additional factor which also has to be taken into account. From the 17th century onwards a form of production developed which yielded large and regular profits, but which was not based on 'free' labour. The slavery on the plantations of the

106

new world could be a very efficient form of production and yield huge and reliable profits, most of which ended up in the hands of the merchant capitalists who supplied the slaves and sold the plantations' products.[134] These profits could give a big boost to capitalist development. But slavery could never supplant free labour as the motor of that development. Slavery was only an efficient method of exploitation in certain cases: where the labour process itself was such as to be easily subject to detailed supervision without much reliance on the initiative of the labourer—as on sugar and cotton plantations—and where the market for the product was virtually guaranteed to expand, so that the owner would not lose money through having to keep his 'property' alive through periods of idle production.

These conditions could apply in the case of certain very important crops, but not to the huge range of different products needed for sustained industrial and agricultural expansion.

It is important to remember that the period was still one in which the demand for the products of industry fluctuated wildly from one time of the year to another and could be badly hit by natural occurrences. In industry, 'the typical unit was small, with numbers of workers fluctuating markedly over the year, varying with the state of demand according to the seasons, at the mercy of water power, affected by floods and droughts'.[135]

'Free labour' was much more profitable for the employers under such conditions than slave labour could ever have been. Both British and French merchant capitalism reaped huge profits from hundreds of thousands of slaves. The growth of the new mode of production would have been much slower without them. But slavery itself was only possible in certain sectors of a much wider international division of labour in which the mode of production based upon the exploitation of 'free labour' predominated. The whole system rested on wage labour, for it was this which gave it its great advantage over previous modes of production.

Between two revolutions

The struggle between the old and the new did not end with the crisis of the 17th century, any more than with the crisis of the 14th century. In Germany, Italy and Bohemia the forces of production declined as old feudal forms of exploitation reconsolidated their hold. In France absolutism under Louis XIV recovered from the upheavals of the late 1640s to establish a stronger base than ever. The monarchy forced the great feudal families to accept centralised control by the state, although this meant that taxation increasingly competed with old feudal payments and dues in creaming off the surplus from peasant production. At the same time, it was able to persuade the richest sections of the bourgeoisie to expend much of their wealth on buying their way into existing society—through paying the monarchy itself for the right to noble status and the old aristocracy for feudal landholdings.

Even in Britain the revolutionary dictatorship of the army under Cromwell gave way to a series of compromises with the great landowners and merchants, the restored monarchy of 1660 and, when this began to show absolutist pretensions, the settlement of 1688. The new groups of exploiters who based themselves on forms of capitalist exploitation, pure or bastardised, urban or rural, were still too weak to impose their will on the rest of society without some reliance on forces below them which they had come to fear,[136] and most were prepared to put their trust in the aristocrats and gentry to keep order. By 1660 their attitude was that without a monarchy there could be no growth of trade.[137]

The defeats and compromises of the mid-17th century did not, however, destroy the trend towards capitalist development. In Britain it proceeded at a steady, if at first slow, pace in town and country for more than 100 years before accelerating massively at the end of the 18th century. The population of London increased 50 percent between 1650 and 1750, so that it became easily the biggest city in Europe.[138] Although 70 to 80 percent of the population still worked in agriculture, it now 'generated no more than 56 percent of the national incomes. Next to agriculture, textiles made the largest contribution to the national income'.[139]

The putting out system still dominated in textiles, but took on increasingly capitalist characteristics as big clothiers advanced at the expense of small ones, so that 'the bulk of workers had no other resources but their labour'.[140] Meanwhile 'more modern modes of production' were to be found in other industries which grew in this period, such as 'brewing, glass manufacture, paper manufacture, refining of salt and sugar...'[141] Symbolic of the changes which were taking place was the growth of coal production as coal replaced wood in 'soap making, brick manufacture, brewing, refining of salt, alum, and sugar and glass making':[142]

In the early decades of the 18th century a seven fold increase occurred in the collier population of the southern area [of Lancashire] and in the maximum size of collieries there... In the third decade in the neighbouring south western area an 'industrial revolution' occurred in mining: massive growth, greatly increased scale of the units of production, technological innovation, increased productivity of labour, capital infusion, and fierce competition...[143]

Across the whole range of industries innovation in terms of new ways of marketing and the production of new commodities was widespread.[144] The invention and spread of new technologies took place at a slower pace. Nevertheless, Schlumbohm can estimate rises in productivity for particular industrial processes ranging from 30 to 1,000 percent.[145]

In agriculture the growth of capitalist methods of exploitation continued at an accelerating pace, here symbolised by the enclosure of land: in Leicestershire only 10 percent of land was enclosed in the 16th century; the crisis of the 17th century increased the pressure on poorer peasants to sell land to the landlords who could then rent it out; and where 'voluntary' methods did not work, compulsion could be used—in 1721-50 there were 100 parliamentary bills of enclosure, 156 in 1750-60, 424 in 1760-70, 642 in 1770-80.[146] The change in the methods of exploitation was accompanied by innovation in farming techniques: farmers responded to the price changes of the crisis years by growing crops like sainfoin, clover and turnips as well as grain, using new systems of rotation which enabled them to keep larger and better nourished herds.[147] The overall productivity of agriculture rose by between 13 and 25 percent,[148] a 'formidable achievement'[149] in a pre-industrial society.

Under French absolutism neither industry nor capitalist agriculture developed nearly as rapidly as in post-revolutionary Britain. As we have seen, the successful merchants very often used their wealth to try to buy their way into the old ruling class. Nevertheless, the shift was not all in one direction. The French bourgeoisie had not been nearly as damaged by the outcome of the wars and civil wars of the 17th century as had the German and Italian bourgeoisies. And the French intelligentsia, including members of the aristocracy and advisers to the monarchy, were as impressed by the ability of the smaller British state to challenge French military might as they were by the superior running of the British economy. McNally shows in detail how the physiocrats, the dominant economic school of mid-18th century France, were concerned with how to push capitalist development forward in overwhelmingly agricultural France[150]—although his reliance on Brenner's ideas leads him to understate the degree to which capitalist development was already occurring in industry and agriculture.

By the end of the 18th century there were a million people involved in the rural textile industry:

> Cloth was the country's foremost export, taking pride of place over grain and wine, enabling France to get the precious metals she herself did not produce... The dispersed yet massive strength of the textile industry played a far more important role than its output (apparently not even 5 percent of the GNP) and the workforce (probably not much more than 5 percent of the population) would suggest.[151]

In addition, shipbuilding, iron and steel, and coal mining all advanced: 'The overall rate of expansion (of industry) must have worked out at 60 percent for the 18th century as a whole'.[152] In a number of regions of the country capitalist and semi-capitalist agriculture began to develop, and with it the adoption of new forms of cultivation.[153]

Contrary to what Brenner argues, France was not moving in the opposite direction to Britain, but in the same direction, at a slower pace. If France seemed relatively backward economically, this was not because it saw no advance in agriculture and industry, but because its global output was only about the same as its British rival which had but a quarter of its population. So it was that France saw the growth of both a big merchant capitalist bourgeoisie and a host of smaller independent producers exploiting a few wage labourers in a capitalist or semi-capitalist manner. So it was that sections of the nobility began to invest in trade and, occasionally, large scale industrial production, just as merchants were investing in land. So it was, too, that a whole ideology could develop within mid-18th century French absolutism which saw capitalist forms of exploitation as more advanced than feudal ones. Braudel has quite correctly summarised the development:

> The whole revolutionary ideology of the enlightenment...was

directed against the privileges of the leisured aristocratic class, defending by contrast, in the name of progress, the active population—including merchants, manufacturers and reforming landowners... The idleness and uselessness of the high and mighty was compared to the industry and social usefulness of the active class.[154]

The French economy entered into a new period of crisis in the 1770s and 1780s. The collaboration between old and new exploiting classes was suddenly subject to the same strains it had experienced throughout Europe in the crisis of the previous century. Once again a section of the old ruling class tried to protect itself by turning society backwards, and once again those associated with the new methods of exploitation were compelled, often despite themselves, to fight. A century and a quarter of continuing economic advance meant that the class alignments in the revolution that followed were less complex than those in the first half of the 17th century. But it still required leadership of genius, this time of the Jacobins, to construct a coalition of forces committed to reorganising society on the basis of the new, capitalist methods, in the face of opposition from those bourgeois interests which had become most incorporated into the old society.

Conclusion

I have attempted to provide an overview of the transition from feudalism to capitalism. Marx's writings should never be regarded as holy writ by Marxists. He never had time to work out many of his ideas, he was quite capable of making mistakes in his reasoning and there have been considerable advances in historical knowledge since his time. But it is worth noting when he was right. In *Capital* he points to a fourfold origin of capitalism: in the growth of trade, in the use of free labour in manufacturing, in separation of the peasantry from the land, and in the 'primitive accumulation of capital'.

For Marx there was an interrelation between the four elements. They all arose from the way in which the growth of the forces of production within feudalism threw up new relations of production, relations which came into collision with the old society when it entered into crisis. These new relations did not displace feudal exploitation immediately, but ensured a longer or shorter transition period, in which periods of peace and even cooperation between old and new exploiting classes were interspersed with bitter conflicts, revolutions and civil wars. This enabled him to see how the bourgeois revolution is centred in the towns but is reinforced by the revolt of the rural classes. It also enabled him to incorporate into his account the insights he had made 20 years before, when in *The German Ideology* he connected the rise of capitalism with the development of the forces of production and when in *The Communist Manifesto* he traced the history of the bourgeoisie back to the medieval towns.

Marx never fully completed his account. As Schlumbohm has correctly noted, 'Marx never really analysed...the inner logic of pre-capitalist and transitional relations of production',[155] and so there are many gaps in his argument that need to be filled. That is no reason to retreat into counterposing one element in his approach to the others, as, in their own ways, both the Pirenne-Sweezy-Wallerstein school and the Brenner school do. Each ends up by revising parts of Marxism: the Pirenne-Sweezy-Wallerstein school by focusing on the 'peoples' of the Third World rather than the international working class; the Brenner school by separating off the struggle between the classes from the material circumstances in which it takes place. Fortunately there is an alternative to both, some elements of which I've tried to outline in this article.

Notes

1   G Comninel, *Rethinking the French Revolution* (London, 1987), p169;
    the quote from Marx is from *Capital*, vol III, p54.
2   S H Rigby, *Marxism and History* (Manchester, 1987), p13.
3   C Barker, *International Socialism* 34, p118.
4   For my understanding of Marx's account, see my article, 'Base and
    Superstructure', ch 1 above.
5   This was true both of the debates in the 1950s occasioned by Maurice
    Dobb's *Studies in the Development of Capitalism* and of the more recent
    debate around the ideas of Robert Brenner.
6   E Pirenne, *Economic and Social History of Medieval Europe* (New York,
    1937), section reprinted in A F Cantor and M S Werthman (eds),
    Medieval Society, 400-1450 (New York, 1972), p132.
7   E Pirenne, op cit, p148.
8   E Pirenne, ibid, p150.
9   R Hilton (ed), *The Transition from Feudalism to Capitalism* (London,
    1982), p42.
10 For summaries of his arguments, see I Wallerstein, *Historical Capitalism*
    (London 1983), pp30-31 and 40-43.
11 See especially, F Braudel, *Capitalism and Civilisation*, vol 2: *The Wheels
    of Commerce* (London, 1982).
12 Although Weber is obsessed by the contrast between the 'rational' pursuit
    of profit under modern capitalism and the less systematic pursuit of it in
    what he sees as previous forms of capitalism.
13 I Wallerstein, op cit, p14.
14 See E Pirenne, *Mohammed and Charlemagne* (London, 1968), pp171-185.
15 I Wallerstein, op cit, p41.
16 This was a point made long ago by Marx, see for instance *Capital*, vol I
    (Moscow, 1961), p715: 'To become a free seller of labour power…he
    [the worker] must have escaped from the regime of the guilds.'
17 K Marx and F Engels, *Collected Works*, vol 30, p36.
18 K Marx and F Engels, *Collected Works*, vol 30, p37.
19 Wallerstein recognises this, but then argues that, because slave production
    in the Americas and feudal production in eastern Europe were for
    markets, they were forms of capitalism!
20 M Dobb, in R Hilton, op cit, p60.
21 Ibid, p59.
22 M Dobb, *Studies…*, p65.
23 In R Hilton, op cit, pp61-62.
24 M Dobb, *Studies…*, p17.
25 Ibid, p20.
26 Ibid, p42.
27 Ibid, p47.
28 M Dobb in R Hilton, op cit, p59.
29 Ibid, p58.
30 K Marx, *Capital*, vol I (Moscow, 1961), p715.
31 R Brenner, 'The Origins of Capitalist Development: a Critique of neo-
    Smithian Marxism', *New Left Review* 104, July-August 1977.
32 The debate in the pages of *Past and Present* over this article is reprinted as
    T H Ashton and C H E Philpin (eds), *The Brenner Debate* (London, 1988).
33 'The Agrarian Roots of European Capitalism', in *The Brenner Debate*, p54.
34 Ibid, p214.
35 What Brenner, by a misleading comparison with the dynamics of
    capitalism, refers to as 'political accumulation'.

36 *The Brenner Debate*, p293.

37 The term is used by Bois, 'Against neo-Malthusian Orthodoxy', ibid, p115, and taken up by E M Wood in *New Left Review* 127, p76. For a full analysis of the current which is identified with it, see A Callinicos, appendix to 'Bourgeois Revolutions and Historical Materialism', *International Socialism* 43.

38 As Bois, one of the contributors to the *Past and Present* debate, quite rightly noted, Brenner's position 'amounts to a voluntarist vision of history in which class struggle is divorced from all objective contingencies and in the first place from such laws of development as may be peculiar to a specific mode of production', *The Brenner Debate*, p115.

39 Indian Marxists have long been vexed by the character of the mode of production in India after the mutiny. The British colonial authorities created a class of rural landowners with legislation modelled on conditions in the British countryside, but the landowners did not begin to adopt methods of capitalist farming until much later—until the inter-war years in the Punjab and until after independence elsewhere. The form of property ownership did not in itself produce capitalist production relations. The argument is very well put by Utsa Patnaik, in Ashoki Rudra and others, *Studies in the Development of Capitalism in India*, (Lahore, 1978), from p53 onwards, who points out that neither the separation of agricultural labourers from the means of production nor the existence of a world market was enough to give rise to capitalist production relations. That required 'the creation of an expanding domestic market owing to large investment outlays by the state'.

40 'Agrarian Class Structure', in *The Brenner Debate*, p39.

41 Ibid, p40

42 Ibid, p40.

43 Summary of Fisher's argument in E A Wrigley, 'London's Importance 1650-1750', in Patten (ed), *Pre-Industrial England, Geographical Essays*, p202.

44 F J Fisher, 'The Development of the London Food Market, 1540-1640', *Economic History Review* V (1934-5), p63, quoted in E A Wrigley, op cit.

45 For a discussion on this question, see Roehl, 'Patterns and Structure of Demand', in C M Cipolla (ed), *The Fontana Economic History of Europe, The Middle Ages*, pp118-119.

46 S Thrupp, 'Medieval Industry, 1000-1500', in C M Cipolla (ed), op cit, p231. Contrast this with Brenner's claim ('The Agrarian Roots...', p241) that 'little of the output of the growing urban centres goes back into production to augment means of production or means of consumption of direct peasant producers'.

47 Medieval Agriculture'. in C M Cipolla (ed), op cit, p192.

48 For the role of small towns, with only 500-2000 inhabitants, see R Hilton, 'Lords, Burgesses and Hucksters', *Past and Present*, November 1982. See also K Marx, *Capital*, vol III, p804.

49 J V Polisensky, *The Thirty Years War* (London, 1974), p52.

50 G Le Goff, 'The Town as an Agent of Civilisation', in C M Cipolla (ed), op cit, p94.

51 Ibid, p79.

52 See R Hilton, 'Lords...'.

53 E A Wrigley, op cit, p192.

54 Ibid, pp196-197.

55 G Le Goff, *Medieval Civilisation*, pp88-89.

56 'The Agrarian Roots...', op cit, p214.

57   J de L Mann, *The Cloth Industry in the West of England, from 1640 to 1880* (Oxford, 1971), p89.
58   Ibid, pp90-91.
59   'The Agrarian Roots…', op cit, p324.
60   'Agrarian Class Structure', in *The Brenner Debate*, p54.
61   In this he sets a trend which is taken further by E M Wood in her 'The Separation of the Economic and the Political in Capitalism', *New Left Review* 127, May-June 1981, and her 'Marxism and the Course of History', *New Left Review* 147, September-October 1984, and further still by Comninel.
62   Despite his criticisms of what he calls the 'Malthusians' he incorporates large chunks of their interpretation into his theory, without seeing how the development of the forces of production alter the impact of rising population over the whole feudal period.
63   This Marx first argued in *The German Ideology* of 1846—although there he did not use the phrase 'relations of production' but rather 'forms of intercourse'. The argument is repeated in the famous Preface to *A Critique of Political Economy* of 1858, in the 1862 preparatory manuscript for *Capital* (vol 30 of K Marx and F Engels, *Collected Works*), and in *Capital* itself.
      In all of them his usage makes it clear that by 'relations of production' he does not just mean class relations—relations of exploitation—but all those new forms of interaction between human beings that are continually being thrown up by changes in methods of production. A failure to grasp this inevitably leads to a failure to see how one mode of production bears within it the seeds of a subsequent mode of production. This is why it is regrettable that in his absolutely justified critique of Comninel in *International Socialism* 43, Alex Callinicos accepts the myth that there is a change in Marx's understanding of historical materialism between *The Gerrnan Ideology* and *Capital*.
64   S Thrupp, 'Medieval Industry 1000-1500', in C M Cipolla (ed), op cit, p225.
65   J C Russell, 'Population in Europe 500-1500', in C M Cipolla (ed), op cit, p25.
66   'The Agrarian Roots…', op cit, p265.
67   White, 'The Expansion of Technology 500-1500', in C M Cipolla (ed), op cit, p143.
68   This is implied by Wood when she argues that 'the formula concerning the contradictions between forces of production and relations of production' is a 'law of capitalist development' and not of pre-capitalist class structures. 'Marxism and Historical Progress', *New Left Review* 147, p102.
69   *Anri-Dühring*, in K Marx and F Engels, *Collected Works*, vol 25, pp146-151. See also pp609-612 and 613-615.
70   Or at least the surplus which came into the hands of the ruling class, see G de Ste Croix, *The Class Struggle in the Ancient Greek World* (London, 1981).
71   G Le Goff, op cit, p3.
72   P Kriedte (ed), *Industrialisation before Industrialisation* (Cambridge 1981), p19.
73   G Duby, *Rural Economy and Country Life in the Medieval West* (London, 1968), p36.
74   Ibid, p49.
75   G Le Goff, *Medieval Civilisation*, p57.
76   Ibid, p59.
77   Ibid, p198.

78   A C Crombie, 'Medieval Science and Technology', in A Cantor and F Werthman, op cit, p240.

79   Ibid, pp232-234; see also G Duby, 'Rural Economy…', op cit, pp88-89.

80   Although proponents of the Brenner thesis should note that the ecclesiastics did attempt from the 10th century onwards to reduce the devastation to society caused by internal warfare with campaigns for 'peace'. See Bloc, *Feudal Society*, pp408-431.

81   Roehl, 'Patterns and Structure of Demands, 1000-1500', in C M Cipolla (ed), op cit, p133.

82   D McNally, paraphrasing Brenner, op cit, p3.

83   For a discussion on what is and what is not known, see the early chapters of G Duby, *Rural Economy and Country Life in the Medieval West* (London, 1968).

84   White, op cit, p146.

85   Ibid, p153. See also G Le Goff, *Medieval Civilisation*, pp54 and 59; and G Duby, 'Medieval Agriculture' in C M Cipolla (ed), op cit, pp176-197.

86   G Duby, op cit, pp195-196.

87   Ibid, p196.

88   G Duby, *Rural Economy…*, op cit, p103.

89   G Le Goff, op cit, pp73-74. See also his accounts of the growth of different towns, pp72, 76, 77.

90   White, in C M Cipolla (ed), op cit, p144.

91   S Thrupp, op cit, p234.

92   G Le Goff, op cit, p74.

93   Ibid, p75.

94   Ibid, p75.

95   Ibid, p75.

96   Holmes, *Europe, Hierarchy and Revolt, 1320-1450* (London, 1975).

97   Quoted ibid, p70. See also P Pieri, *Il Rinascimento e la Crisi Militare Italiana* (Einaudi, 1952), p50.

98   I should say, 'almost all the debates', since Brenner virtually ignores it.

99   The example of the latifundia and slave plantations has been well documented: See, for example, E Williams, *Capitalism and Slavery*. For the causes behind the rise of Stalin's labour camps, see T Cliff, *State Capitalism in Russia* (London, 1988).

100   *Capital*, vol I (Moscow, 1961), p715.

101   In P Kriedte (ed), op cit.

102   J Schlumbohm, op cit, p111.

103   P Kriedte, in P Kriedte (ed), op cit.

104   Ibid, p34.

105   Ibid, p33.

106   J Schlumbohm, in Kriedte (ed), op cit, pp95-96.

107   P Kriedte, in P Kriedte (ed), op cit, p29.

108   P Kriedte, *Peasants, Landlords and Merchant Capitalists* (Leamington Spa, 1987), p41.

109   R Hilton, 'Lords, Burgesses and Hucksters', *Past and Present*, November 1982.

110   G Duby, in C M Cipolla (ed), op cit, p193.

111   G Duby, *Rural Economy…*, op cit, p165 .

112   Ibid, p151.

113   Ibid, pp96-97.

114   Ibid, p193.

115   G Le Goff, in C M Cipolla (ed), op cit, p94.

116   See P Kriedte, *Peasants…*, op cit, p90.

117   G Le Goff, *Medieval Civilisation*, op cit, p95.

118 G Duby, *Rural Economy...*, op cit, p165.
119 Ibid, p165.
120 M Dobb, *Studies...*, op cit, and P Anderson, *Lineages of the Absolute State* (London, 1974), pp18-19.
121 P Sweezy in R Hilton (ed), op cit.
122 Holmes, op cit, p116.
123 P Anderson, op cit, pp21-22.
124 As Anderson puts it earlier, op cit, pp18 and 20.
125 *Origins of the Family*, quoted in P Anderson p15.
126 For a summary of these revolts see Holmes, op cit, pp125-133.
127 Ibid, p133.
128 Brenner's own account, in terms of traditional peasant solidarity. is unconvincing, as Heidi Wunder shows, in *The Brenner Debate*, pp91-100, although she provides no real account of her own.
129 As when the Parisian bourgeoisie, involved in a dispute of its own with the feudal ruling class, vacillated over whether to support the peasant rebellion of 1378 and, in effect, allowed the feudal forces to crush it. See Holmes, op cit, p41.
130 For an excellent account of the economic roots of the Bohemian revolt, see J V Polisensky, *The Thirty Years War* (London, 1974), pp37-39, 41, and 47-50.
131 Ibid, p17.
132 Ibid, p17.
133 P Kriedte, op cit, p 90.
134 See, for instance, the calculations in R W Fogel and S L Engelmen, *Time on the Cross* (London, 1974).
135 D C Coleman, *Industry in Tudor and Stuart England* (London, 1975), p36.
136 For an account of how the lower classes mobilised see B Manning, *The English People and the English Revolution* (London, 1976). See also virtually any of the writings of C Hill, especially, *The World Turned Upside Down*.
137 C Hill, *Milton and the English Revolution* (London 1977), p186.
138 E A Wrigley, op cit, p203.
139 P Kriedte, *Peasants...*, op cit, p77.
140 J de L Mann, *The Cloth Industry in the West of England* (Oxford, 1971), p102.
141 P Kriedte, *Peasants...*, op cit, p78.
142 Ibid, p78.
143 Langston, 'Coal Output in South West Lancashire, 1590-1799', in Patten, op cit, p242.
144 See, for instance, J de L Mann, op cit, ch 1.
145 J Schlumbohm, in P Kriedte (ed), op cit, p111.
146 P Kriedte, *Peasants...*, op cit, pp106-107.
147 Ibid, p68.
148 Estimates quoted in E A Wrigley, op cit, p204.
149 Ibid.
150 A point which Marx made in those notebooks for *Capital* which are published under the title *Theories of Surplus Value*.
151 Goubert, *The Ancien Regime* (London, 1973), p57.
152 Ibid, p57.
153 Ibid, pp113-115.
154 F Braudel, *Capitalism and Civilisation*, vol 2, *The Wheels of Commerce* (London, 1982), p504.
155 J Schlumbohm, op cit, p74.